How To Design and Construct a Power Boat

by The Rudder Magazine

with an introduction by Roger Chambers

Self Reliance Books

Get more historic titles on animal and stock breeding, gardening and old fashioned skills by visiting us at:

http://selfreliancebooks.blogspot.com/

Introduction

I am pleased to present another book in the "Boat" series.

The work is in the Public Domain and is re-printed here in accordance with Federal Laws.

As with all reprinted books of this age that are intended to perfectly reproduce the original edition, considerable pains and effort had to be undertaken to correct fading and sometimes outright damage to existing proofs of this title. At times, this task is quite monumental, requiring an almost total "rebuilding" of some pages from digital proofs of multiple copies. Despite this, imperfections still sometimes exist in the final proof and may detract from the visual appearance of the text.

I hope you enjoy reading this book as much as I enjoyed making it available to readers again.

With Regards,

Roger Chambers

Preface

THE small launch driven by steam that was used in the days of our fathers was an unhandy and to an extent dangerous contrivance. With the exception of a few built especially for sea-going, these craft were crank and wet, owing to the high weights and lean lines. The modern power-driven craft is a very different vessel, the best of them being able, seaworthy boats, capable of being driven anywhere a small ship can go. The best of these modern boats is that type known as the hunting cabin. This type is a direct descendant of the Cape Cod cabin cat, its original ancestor being a boat of that type belonging to a New York man, who, in the early days of the gasolene engine placed one of these machines in it.

The popularity of this type and its widespread acceptance is due largely to the efforts of THE RUDDER, which magazine took up and advocated the model, and subsequently encouraged the improvement by inaugurating long-distance sea-course racing. The first plans of this type were published in THE RUDDER and circulated world-wide, and to-day there are no yachting people but what are building and using the hunting cabin launch.

The first requisite in these boats is safety, the second comfort, and the third speed. Consequently, where the designer has observed this succession of requirements he has produced a serviceable and seaworthy craft; where he has violated it by putting speed first the boats have been either failures or disappointments in performance.

The first essential of seaworthiness and comfort is width. A narrow boat is always a wet and uncomfortable craft, and is lacking of room, nor is there any compensating advantage in narrow craft for the general purposes of yachting, as high speed is not so much the result of narrowing a hull as it is the absence of weight. And weight is of material consequence in all boats designed for general use and cruising service. Rigidity of hull is essential to seaworthiness, and such rigidity cannot be obtained and kept unless considerable weight is put into a vessel.

The hunting cabin type used as an example in this work, is not a suitable type for boats over fifty feet top measure—the best boats are those from thirty to forty feet—and we do not recommend the young designer and builder to build one of these craft of more than forty feet extreme length. For such a boat the extreme limit of speed is set at about ten miles, and to attempt to drive it faster would be a waste of power. The result of racing this type of boat over long distances has shown that low-speed engines give the best results and are the most economical in fuel consumption, requiring less tankage for the miles covered—an item of importance when a boat is to be used for cruising.   EDITOR.

Its Design and Construction

THE subject of naval architecture, as applied to the design of yachts, is one of the most fascinating and absorbing studies that it is possible to take up; and a study it is, as you are continually encountering new difficulties at each step which, together with the improvements and discoveries of others, compel you to study until you lay aside your pen and pencil forever. As with art and poetry, so it is with naval architecture; you must be able to see the finished product before starting to paint, write or draw a line. The artist must have pictured in his mind just what his picture will look like, otherwise it would not be possible to paint it at all. Imagine, if you can, an artist starting to paint a picture that he had no idea what it would look like when finished. So it is in the design of a yacht; one must have every detail fixed in his mind before starting to draw, or the first thing he knows he will have the bow of one boat and the stern of another with the usual result—failure.

In the design of yachts it is necessary to possess a certain knowledge of mathematics, otherwise it would not be possible for the designer to perform the necessary calculations that enter into every design.

It is probably time for me to say that this article is not to be a thoroughly scientific article on naval architecture, but merely a treatise covering the subject as far as to enable one to calculate the displacement, weight and center of buoyancy of a given design, together with a chapter on resistance and powering, thereby giving the owner of a power boat a chance to become better acquainted with his boat, and to be able perhaps to remedy some slight defect that he might find in her whereby he would improve the speed or seaworthiness of his yacht.

It is unnecessary to go into the calculations for stability of the ordinary launch of forty feet and under, and as this is the size I propose to treat I will eliminate these calculations.

The method used to express a rule for calculating is called a formula, and is used because it is much more convenient. Any formula can be expressed in words, and when so expressed becomes a rule. Formulas, however, are much to be preferred, as they show at a glance all the operations that are to be performed, and do not require to be read over three or four times, as is the case with most rules, to enable one to understand their meaning.

The majority of calculations that fall to the lot of the designer consist of determining the area and position of center of gravity of various shaped figures. The area of a square or rectangular figure in feet is equal to the length of one side in feet multiplied by the other side

Irene. Dimensions—Length O. A. 33 Ft., Length W. L. 29.10 Ft., Breadth Extreme 8.6 Ft., Breadth W. L. 7.6 Ft., Draught 3 Ft., Freeboard, Bow 4.9 Ft., Freeboard, Least 2.9 Ft., Freeboard, Stern 2.8 Ft.

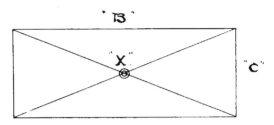

in feet, while the center of gravity would be a point formed by the intersection of two lines drawn from the opposite corners, as shown at X. The algebraic formula, as it is called, for calculating the area would be $A = B \times C = A = 12 \times 5 = 60$ square feet. The area or quantity to be obtained being represented by the letter A.

The area of a triangle is equal to the base multiplied by the perpendicular height and the result divided by 2—thus:

$$A = \frac{B \times C}{2} = A = \frac{7 \times 5}{2} = \frac{35}{2} = 1.75 \text{ square feet.}$$

To find the center of gravity of a triangle: bisect each side and draw a line to the opposite corner—thus: The intersection of the three lines will be the C. G., or center of gravity.

The area of a circle is equal to $D^2 \times .7854$. Thus the area of a circle 2 feet in diameter would be

$$2^2 \times .7854 = 4 \times .7854 = 3.1416 \text{ square feet.}$$

To find the circumference, multiply the diameter by 3.1416. To find the diameter divide the circumference by 3.1416.

To find the area of a quadrilateral having no two sides equal divide it into two triangles, calculate the area of each and add together the results—thus:

$$A = \frac{U \times S}{2} + \frac{T \times S}{2} = \frac{5 \times 10}{2} + \frac{4 \times 10}{2} = 25 + 20 = 45$$

square feet.

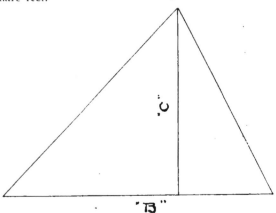

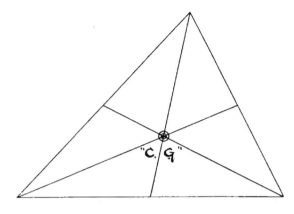

To find the center of gravity draw the lines A B and C D; measure on C D from C the distance D E. This new point call F, and draw the lines F A and F B. This gives you a triangle formed by A B F. Bisect F B, F A and A B and draw lines from G to A, H to B and

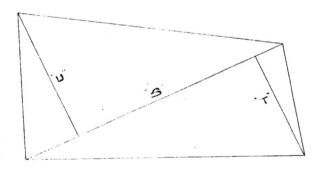

I to F. The intersection of these will be the center of gravity of the whole figure.

To find the cubical contents or volume of a body having three dimensions multiply the height by the width and the result by the length—thus:

$$V. = H \times W \times L = 4 \times 3 \times 7 = 84 \text{ cubic feet.}$$

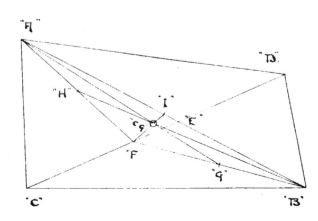

DISPLACEMENT

The displacement of any floating body, whether a log, barrel, piece of lumber or yacht, is simply the amount of water forced or pushed aside by the body immersed. This law, as it is called, was first discovered by Archi-

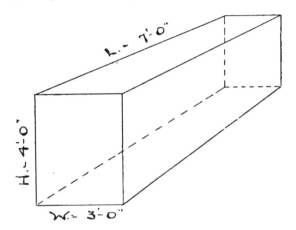

medes, a Greek philosopher, and the fact is known as the Archimedean law: *All bodies on being immersed in a liquid push aside a volume of the liquid equal in weight to the weight of the body immersed.* From this it is evident that the depth to which a body will be immersed in a fluid will depend entirely on the density of the fluid, and it is this fact that makes a vessel draw less in salt water than in fresh. It is from this principle that we are enabled to arrive at the exact weight of a vessel,

because it is obvious that if you can determine the number of cubic feet, or volume, in the immersed body of a vessel, then, as we know that a cubic foot of salt water weighs 64 lb, it is an easy matter to obtain the weight or displacement of the vessel by multiplying the number of cubic feet by 64, which result would give us the weight of the vessel in pounds; or should we desire to obtain the weight or displacement of the vessel in tons it would be necessary to divide the number of cubic feet or volume in the immersed body by 35, as there are 35 cubic feet of water to a ton. (In all cases a ton is measured as 2,240 lb. This may be readily proved by multiplying 35 × 64 = 2,240 lb.)

If the vessel were of box form or shape it would be a simple matter to calculate the immersed area by multiplying the length by breadth by draught, but as the immersed body of a yacht is of curvilinear form the problem resolves itself into one requiring the application of one of a number of methods of calculation, the principal one being known as Simpson's Rule.

The calculation of an area such as shown is usually defined as follows: Divide the base line A B into an even number of parts and erect perpendicular ordinates, as they are called, Y1, Y2, etc., from the base line to the curve, and after measuring off the lengths of these ordinates, to the sum of the first and last ordinate add four times the even ordinates and twice the odd ordinates. Multiply the sum total by one-third of the common interval X between the ordinates and the result will be the

Vidofuer. Dimensions—Length O. A. 58.3 Ft., Length W. L. 53.8 Ft., Breadth 11 Ft., Draught 3.4 Ft.

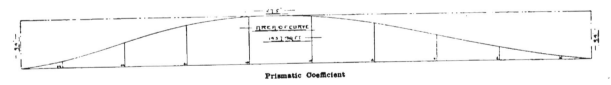

Prismatic Coefficient

In laying out a curve of versed sines draw a semicircle in which A B equals the area of your amidship section. Divide the semicircle into 4 equal parts and draw lines from the center to the points 1, 2 and 3. Divide the base line B C into the same number of parts and erect perpendiculars from 1B, 2B and 3B. Now draw lines from the points 1, 2 and 3 parallel to the base line until they intersect the lines 1B, 2B and 3B, and through the intersections, 1A, 2A and 3A, draw the line A C, which will be a curve of versed sines. The area of the curve is exactly one-half of a circumscribing parallelogram and consequently has a coefficient of .5. A trochoidal curve is constructed in much the same way as a curve of versed sines in that you draw a semicircle whose diameter A B equals the area of your midsection, after which it is divided into four parts as shown and lines drawn from

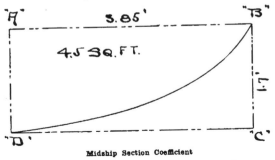

Midship Section Coefficient

B to 1, 2, 3. Divide the base line B C into four equal parts and draw 1.A 1.C parallel to 1.B; 2.A 2.C parallel to 2.B; and 3.A 3.C parallel to 3.B. Now draw 1.A 1 parallel to B C; 2.A 2 parallel to B C, and 3.A 3 parallel to B C, and draw a line through the intersections A, 1.A, 2.A, 3.A and C, which will give you a trochoidal curve. In laying down a curve of areas for a boat it does not follow that you must design the boat to the curve but that the curve merely acts as a guide, for as a matter of fact the forebody of most launches is somewhat fuller than a curve of versed sines. The relation that the area of a curve of areas bears to a circumscribing parallelogram is known as the prismatic coefficient, and by this coefficient you can tell whether a boat is full lined or not.

Suppose you had a boat 40 feet on the water-line with a midship section area of 12 sq. ft.; this would give you an area of 40 × 12 = 480 cu. ft. If the actual displacement of this boat were 16,000 ℔ the cubic area of its underwater body would be $\frac{16000}{64}$ = 250 cubic feet.

Now knowing these facts it is an easy matter to determine the prismatic coefficient by dividing 480 into 250, or $\frac{250}{480}$ = .52+. Thus she would have a P. C. of .52+.

The P. C. varies considerably with different types of boats, the average, however, being from .50 to .60 per cent. Suppose in the boat just considered you desired to make the coefficient .57 and in order to do so it is of course necessary to reduce the area of the midship section; but the question arises, how much? This may be obtained in the following manner:

Let A = area of M. S.,
D = displacement in cubic feet,
L = length of l. w. l.,
P = prismatic coefficient,

then we have—

$$A = \frac{D}{L\,P} = \frac{250}{40 \times .57} = \frac{250}{22.8} = 10.965 \text{ square feet, area}$$

of M. S. This may be readily proved by reversing the formula:

$$10.965 \times 40 \times .57 = 250 \text{ square feet.}$$

After all that has been said regarding the wave-form theory, this of itself will not produce a speedy or successful design, as many successful yachts have been built having a curve very different from that prescribed by the theory; likewise many unsuccessful yachts have been designed that conformed closely to the wave-line theory. There is no doubt, however, but that there is a decided advantage in having the area curve conform closely to the wave-form theory. Still, its importance should not be overestimated. In addition to the P. C. there are two other coefficients that are taken into consideration in designing a yacht; viz., the block coefficient and the midship section coefficient.

The block coefficient of fineness, as it is called, is that ratio that the finished immersed body or volume of displacement bears to a block having the same length as the load water-line, the same breadth, at load water-line and the same draught, to rabbet line. Thus the yacht considered with breadth of 9 feet and draught of 2 feet would have a block area of $40 \times 9 \times 2 = 720$ cubic feet, and as the actual volume of displacement was 250 cubic feet the block coefficient of fineness would be $\frac{250}{720}$ $= .347$. In other words in cutting a model you would cut away .653% of the wood and have only .347% left. This coefficient gives a very good idea of the fineness of a yacht and is of value in determining the approximate displacement of other yachts of about the same size and type.

The midship section coefficient is that ratio that the area of the M. S. bears to a rectangle whose breadth is equal to the breadth of the M. S. at the load water-line and whose depth is equal to the draught at the rabbet line. Thus the yacht just considered had a breadth of 9 feet and draught of 2 feet, therefore a rectangle of this size would contain $9 \times 2 = 18$ square feet. The actual area being 12 square feet the midship section coefficient of fineness would be $\frac{12}{18} = .667$.

Center of Buoyancy

The center of buoyancy (C. B.) is simply the exact center of the volume of the water displaced by a vessel, or its center of gravity, and its location below the load water-line is regulated by the form of the immersed body. If your boat has considerable dead-rise it will be of course nearer the surface than if the bilge was low and hard. Its fore-and-aft position must of necessity be in the middle line plane of the yacht, as both sides are alike. To determine the fore-and-aft position, take the areas of the sections and put them through Simpson's Rule, using the example previously used; these functions of areas are in turn multiplied by the interval, each one being multiplied by the number of intervals they respectively are from No. 1. Divide the sum of these moments by the sum of the functions and multiply the result by 4, as you have only multiplied by the number of intervals away and not by the distance, which in this case is 4 feet.

Ord.	Area	Mult.	Funct.	Interval	Moments
Y1 =	2	1	2	0	0
Y2 =	3	4	12	1	12
Y3 =	4	2	8	2	16
Y4 =	7	4	28	3	84
Y5 =	5	2	10	4	40
Y6 =	4	4	16	5	80
Y7 =	3	1	3	6	18
			79		250

$\frac{250}{79} = 3.164 \times 4 = 12.656$ feet, C. B. is aft of Y1.

Assuming that this is the calculation of an actual yacht the position of the C. B. would be 12.656 feet aft of Y1, which would be the forward end of the load water-line. As we have 6 even parts of 4 feet each, we must have a water-line length of $6 \times 4 = 24$ feet, and as the C. B. is 12.656, its fore-and-aft position is $\frac{12.656}{24} =$ .527%, or a little over 6-10 of a foot aft of the center of the yacht. (A complete calculation of an actual design will be given in the chapter on design.)

To obtain the vertical C. B. take the immersed body and draw in a number of water-lines at equal intervals from the load water-line to the rabbet, obtain their areas and sum up their moments in the same manner as for the fore-and-aft position.

The exact position for the C. B. is something that must be determined by practical experience, the same as with the disposition of the displacement. In the best designs, however, its position will be found between .50 and .55% from the forward end of the load water-line, and in making a design the disposition of the weights must be such as to bring the center of gravity of the whole boat in line with the C. B., or otherwise the yacht when afloat will be either down by the head or by the stern.

Very frequently one will meet with a launch that has a tendency to settle at the stern, or squat as it is called, when underway. This fault is seldom seen where a boat is driven at a speed of less than twice the square root of her water-line length, and where seen to settle at higher rates of speed it can usually be laid to faulty design. This settling may be from various causes, such as having the C. B. in the wrong position, insufficient displacement in the afterbody, too much flare at the water-line forward, or by having the engine and weights too far aft.

A boat is very often said to settle at the stern when there is no settling at all, as, for instance, a boat that has a compromise stern will carry a wave halfway up to the deck at the stern, but if the boat is on her designed water-line forward she is not settling, for if she were she would lift her bow in proportion to what she settled at the stern.

TRIM

In order to secure a perfect fore-and-aft trim of your yacht, it is necessary to so dispose of your weights that the common center of gravity of the whole boat is directly in line with the center of buoyancy, as otherwise she will trim by the head or by the stern as the case may be. In a small launch, however, it is not always possible to so dispose of your weights without a great sac-

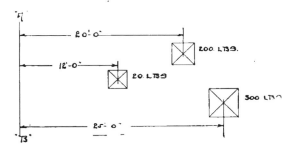

rifice in accommodations, and in such cases it is better to trim the boat by a little ballast rather than spoil the cabin layout. This is very common practice, as the amount of ballast required in so small a boat does not, to any great extent, interfere with its speed.

A complete calculation for the center of gravity is a long and tedious job, as it necessitates a calculation of the weights of all the material entering into the build-ing and equipping of a boat, together with engines, tanks, fuel, water, anchors, cables, etc.

The center of gravity of any number of weights is equal to the sum of their moments divided by the sum of the weights. This will give you the center of gravity of the weights from the point about which moments are taken. Thus, the C. G. of the following weights would be:

Lb.		Arm		Moments
200	×	20	=	4,000
20	×	12	=	240
300	×	25	=	7,500
520				11,740

$$\frac{11,740}{520} = 22.577 \text{ feet C. G.}$$

from line A. B., from which point moments were taken. Now supposing you desired to find the C. G. of a 30-foot water-line design and you had found the weights and C. G. of the various parts in relation to the forward end of the water-line, and found the weights and arm as follows:

	Lb.	Arm	Moments
Hull	4,200	16	67,200
Engine	1,400	20	28,000
Fuel	550	6	3,300
Water	400	25	10,000

Aranca. Dimensions—Length O. A. 36 Ft., Length W. L. 33.10 Ft., Breadth 10.7 Ft., Draught 3 Ft.

	Lb.	Arm	Moments
Cabin	1,000	10	10,000
Cockpit ...	750	27	20,250
Anchors, etc.	200	4	800
	8,500		139,500

Then the C. G. of the whole would be

$$\frac{139.550}{8,500} = 16.416 \text{ feet}$$

aft of the forward end of the L. W. L., or

$$\frac{16.416}{30} = .545\%,$$

which would bring it just about on a line with the C. B. of a launch, or a little aft, of the ordinary type, and in this case would require a very small amount of ballast to trim, as the boat would be a little by the stern.

RESISTANCE

The resistance to a vessel moving through the water may be divided into three parts, viz.:

1. Resistance due to friction of water upon the hull.
2. Resistance due to eddy making.
3. Resistance due to wave making.

The resistance due to friction of water upon the hull, or frictional resistance as it is sometimes called, explains itself. It is of course obvious that a yacht will move through the water at the same speed with less power or at a greater speed with the same power when the bottom is perfectly smooth and clean than it will when covered with marine growth such as grass and barnacles, so that it is essential, if you wish to obtain the best results, to have the bottom free and clean and to have it properly planed so that there are no rough places left in the planks. The frictional resistance forms a larger proportion of the total resistance at slow speeds than it does at higher speeds. Resistance due to eddy making is not so serious in small launches as it is in larger vessels, and generally appears at the after ends of the dead-wood when it is left thick and also at the after ends of struts and rudders. To offset this the dead-wood should be faired off so that the after edge comes to a point, the fairing being done for various distances depending on the shape and thickness of the dead-wood. Struts when used should also be designed with the after end sharp and the forward end well rounded, or eddies will appear at that point. The after edges of rudders where they are of wood should be as thin as possible.

In auxiliaries the eddy making is considerable at the aperture, due chiefly to the extreme thickness of the dead-wood and also to the fact that the hole is cut as small as possible so as not to interfere with the steering and maneuvering of the yacht when under sail. The resistance due to eddy making, however, forms a very small proportion of the total in well-formed yachts.

The resistance due to wave making for low speeds is not experienced to any great extent, but for every yacht there is a certain speed above which the resistance increases more rapidly than would be the case if surface friction and eddy making alone caused the resistance. This extra resistance is caused by the formation of waves upon the surface of the water. It is this resistance that is almost always overlooked by the small boat-builder as well as the small boat owner, with the result that more than half, and you might say with comparative safety four-fifths, of the small power boats are overpowered, which results in an excessive consumption of fuel from which the owner is deriving no benefit whatever. I have often heard the ridiculous argument put forward that by doubling the horse-power in a given launch you should double the speed; and when you take that into consideration, is it any wonder that launches are overpowered and owners disappointed?

It is not my purpose to deal further with the subject of resistance, as it is a subject requiring too much space to permit of a thorough discussion of it here.

PROPULSION OF YACHTS

To propel a yacht through the water some kind of positive thrust must be obtained. This may be had in various ways, as by poling along a shallow body of water, by oars, or by the screw propeller or paddle-wheel, the latter two being by far the most common. In all cases except the first mentioned, the stream of water projected from the vessel propels the vessel by its reaction.

The paddle-wheel is perhaps the most common, or I should say the simplest form, consisting as it does of two rings secured by arms to a hub keyed on a shaft. At the outer edges of the rings and placed between them are wooden paddles or buckets, generally of rectangular form and located equidistant in planes passing through the axis of the shaft. Such wheels are known as radial wheels, and are attached to a hull in such a position that the lower part of the wheel is immersed in the water, to a certain depth, which is known as the dip of the wheel, while the vertical distance from the inner edge of the buckets to the surface of the water is called the immersion of the buckets.

It is of course obvious that when the wheels revolve

the buckets propel a volume of water in the same general direction in which the lower part of the wheel is moving. If you assume the yacht to be at rest with respect to the water in which she floats, before she can move her inertia must be overcome; and before this is done the velocity of the stream of water projected by the buckets is equal in respect to the vessel as well as to the surrounding water. If the stream is projected at a velocity constant in regard to the yacht, as soon as the inertia of the yacht is overcome and she gathers headway the velocity of the stream in regard to the surrounding water will become less until it finally reaches a point where the velocity of the yacht will not increase any more. The difference between the velocity of the stream and the velocity of the vessel is called the slip, and is usually expressed in per cent of the velocity of the stream in regard to the vessel. The formula for calculating slip is as follows:

S = per cent of slip,
V = velocity of stream,
K = velocity of vessel,

then

$$S = 100 \times \frac{V - K}{V}.$$

If a yacht travels 500 feet per minute, with a velocity of stream, in regard to the vessel projected by the paddle-wheel, 700 feet per minute, you have

$$S = 100 \times \frac{700 - 500}{700} = 28.57\% \text{ slip.}$$

By this is determined the efficiency of the propelling instrument, be it wheel, propeller or any other method. It is, of course, evident that for equal speeds and conditions of the same boat, the less the slip the more efficient is the propeller, and the greater the slip the less the efficiency. Furthermore, assuming the efficiency of the propelling instrument to be constant at various speeds, the slip must be greater at higher than at lower speeds, in order to keep the percentage of slip constant.

In order to determine the velocity at which a stream of water is projected by a paddle-wheel, it is necessary to first find the point of the wheel at which its whole action on the water may be assumed to be concentrated. This point is known as the center of pressure of the wheel, and twice the distance of this point from the outer edge of the buckets subtracted from the diameter of the wheel, measured from the outer edge to outer edge of buckets, constitutes the effective diameter of the wheel.

Then if

P = distance, in inches, of center of pressure from the outer edge of buckets;
D = mean depth, in inches, of buckets wholly immersed;
N = number of buckets wholly immersed;
M = mean depth, in inches, of buckets partially immersed;
I = number of buckets partially immersed;

we have

$$P = \frac{D N + M I}{3 (N + I)}.$$

Then if a wheel 4 feet in diameter has, at a certain dip, four buckets of a mean depth of 6 inches, wholly immersed, and one immersed to a depth of 2 inches, we have

$$P = \frac{6 \times 4 + 2 \times 1}{3 (4 + 1)} = 1.733 \text{ inches,}$$

Elkhorn. Dimensions—Length O. A. 102 Ft., Length W. L. 94.6 Ft., Breadth 14 Ft., Draught 5 Ft.

the distance of the center of pressure from the outer edge of the buckets. The diameter of the wheel being 4 × 12 = 48 inches, then the effective diameter is 48 — (2 × 1.733) = 44.534 inches.

This formula is only an approximate one, the exact point not being definitely known and can only be determined by the aid of extended experimental investigation. In the absence of such, it is sufficient for all practical purposes to take it at the center of the buckets, which in this case would make the effective diameter 48 — (2 × 3) = 42 inches, making a difference of 2.534 inches.

Assuming an effective diameter of 42 inches the circumference of the wheel would be 42 × 3.1416 = 131.947 inches, then with the wheel turning at 50 revolutions per minute the speed of a point on the effective diameter circle would be

$$\frac{131.947 \times 50}{12} = \frac{6597.35}{12} = 549.79 \text{ feet}$$

per minute which, without taking into consideration slip, would mean a distance of 32,988 feet in one hour or 6.247 miles.

If, however, the boat to which this wheel was attached had a speed of 449.79 feet per minute, the slip of the wheel would then be

$$P = 100 \times \frac{V - K}{V} = \frac{549.79 - 449.79}{549.79} = 18 + \%$$

The circle whose circumference is equal to the distance traveled, per revolution, is sometimes known as the rolling circle. It is so called from the fact that the speed of the boat is the same as though it were carried on wheels of this diameter which rolled on a road, as carriage wheels. Its diameter may be found by the following rule, in which

V = distance moved by the boat in feet,
R = number of revolutions,
D = diameter of rolling circle,

then

$$D = \frac{V}{3.1416 \text{ R}},$$

and by using the previous example, we have

$$D = \frac{449.79}{3.1416 \times 50} = 2.86 \text{ feet},$$

the diameter of the rolling circle. From this the slip would be the difference between the diameter of the rolling circle and the effective diameter multiplied by 100 and divided by the effective diameter, or 42 inches = 3.5 feet; 3.5 — 2.86 = .64 feet, then

$$S = \frac{.64 \times 100}{3.5} = 18 + \%$$

the same as above.

THE SCREW PROPELLER

If a point be caused to rotate at a uniform distance from and about an axis, and if the point at the same time be caused to advance at a uniform rate in the direction of the axis, its path will be a helix, and if the point, when moving away from the observer, moves in the direction of the hands of a watch, the helix will be right-handed, and if in an opposite direction, left-handed. The distance the point advances in one complete

Mawagra II. Dimensions—Length O. A. 51.6 Ft., Length W. L. 49 Ft., Breadth 10.8 Ft., Draught 3.6 Ft.

revolution is known as the pitch. If a line passing through the axis be caused to rotate about the axis, and to pass along the path of the point mentioned, its path will be the surface of a true screw, provided the angle which the line makes with the axis remains constant. From this it follows that a true screw is one in which the advance of any point, in the direction of the axis, at any distance from it for any part of a revolution is the same. By causing lines making equal angles with each other and the axis, to rotate about the axis in a helical path, a multiple-threaded true screw will be generated having the same pitch as a single-threaded true screw.

Sometimes screw propellers are found, the surface of the blades of which are not truly helical. As usually found, the pitch near the tip is greater than it is near the hub. Such propellers have what is called a radially expanded pitch. The reason for constructing the blade in this manner is that since part of the blade near the hub strikes at nearly a right angle, it acts chiefly to churn the water, thereby causing the tip of the blades to act upon water already in motion; but by increasing the pitch at the tip, it is supposed that the resistance at all parts of the blade is more nearly equalized.

Sometimes the blades are constructed in such a manner that the leading portion of the blade has a finer pitch than the following portion. Such a blade is said to have an expanding pitch. The object aimed at in an expanding pitch is practically the same as in a radially expanded pitch blades are supposed to equalize the resistance at different parts of the blade at varying distances from the axis, expanding pitch blades are supposed to equalize the resistance at different parts of the blade at the same distance from its axis. Neither radially nor expanding pitch screw propellers seem to have met with the success claimed for them, and, while they were in great favor some years ago, at the present time most boats are fitted with propellers having what is commonly known as a true screw.

The blades of a screw propeller drive a stream of water astern, when the propeller is revolving, by their oblique action on the water, and the velocity of the stream is commonly assumed to be that found by multiplying the pitch by the number of revolutions within a certain time. If the distance moved by the boat in the same length of time is known, the slip may be calculated in the same manner as for the paddle-wheel. This slip is not the true slip, but what is known as apparent slip, it being practically impossible to calculate the true slip.

It sometimes occurs in testing propeller wheels that the boat appears to travel faster than the screw. It is of course easy to say that such a thing is impossible, and when this occurs the wheel is said to have a negative slip.

U. S. L. S. S.

Numerous explanations have been given of the phenomenon of apparent negative slip, but none of them can be accepted as satisfactorily accounting for its occurrence in the case of well-formed uniform pitch screws. It has been suggested that the blades twist or spring under pressure of the water, which would have the effect of increasing the pitch, and that they recover their shape when the pressure is relieved, so that measurements taken after the trial would even be misleading. If, however, this were the case, screws with thin blades would be most likely to show apparent negative slip, but it is, on the contrary, generally met with in screws with very thick blades where springing would be least likely to occur.

It has also been suggested that if a boat having a blunt stern moves through the water at a high rate of speed, the surrounding water is not able to flow in along the sides of the vessel sufficiently rapid to fill in at the stern, and that the water from the sides must flow in in order to fill the channel, as it were, formed by the boat in passing through the water. This means that a column of water is following the boat, and whenever apparent negative slip has been observed it has always been accompanied with a great waste of power.

The pitch, as has been previously defined, is the distance which a propeller in one revolution would drive the boat if it worked on an unyielding surface. Such, however, is not the case and, in consequence, the water recedes somewhat under the action of the propeller and the boat moves forward a distance less than the pitch. The difference between the pitch and the distance traveled by the boat is known as the slip and is expressed as a per cent.

In order to determine the slip ratio or slip we have,

Let P = pitch of propeller in feet,

N = revolutions per minute,

V = velocity of boat in knots,

S = slip ratio,

101.3 = a constant,

then

$$S = \frac{P - \frac{101.3\,V}{N}}{P}.$$

Suppose you have a boat with a wheel having a 3-foot pitch, turning at 350 revolutions per minute and giving the boat a speed of 8 knots per hour, then

$$S = \frac{3 - \frac{101.3 \times 8}{.350}}{3} = \frac{3 - 2.3154}{3} = \frac{.6846}{3}\ 22.8\%\ \text{slip};$$

$$\text{or, } S = \frac{P\,N - 101.3\,V}{P\,N} = \frac{3 \times 350 - 101.3 \times 8}{3 \times 350} =$$

$$\frac{1050 - 810.4}{1050} = \frac{239.6}{1050} = 22.8\%.$$

Desired the speed, knowing the pitch, revolutions and slip, we have

$$V = \frac{P\,N\,(1 - S)}{101.3} = \frac{3 \times 350\,(1 - .228)}{101.3} = \frac{1050 \times .772}{101.3} =$$

$$\frac{810.6}{101.3} = 8\ \text{knots}.$$

Desired the number of revolutions, having the other items, then

Augusta II. Dimensions—Length O. A. 76.8 Ft., Length W. L. 70 Ft., Breadth 11.9 Ft., Draught 3 10 Ft.

A. C. Dimensions—Length O. A. 45 Ft., Length W. L. 43 Ft., Breadth 9 Ft., Draught 3 Ft.

$$N = \frac{101.3\ V}{P(1-S)} = \frac{101.3 \times 8}{3 \times .772} = \frac{810.4}{2.316} = 350 \text{ revolutions.}$$

Desired the pitch, having the other items, then

$$P = \frac{101.3\ V}{(N\ 1-S)} = \frac{810.4}{270.2} = 3.0 \text{ feet.}$$

POWERING

The subject of the powering of boats will only be referred to in a general way, as was the subject of propulsion. The usual problems in this connection are to find the power required to drive a boat at a certain speed, and the speed a boat will have with a given horse-power. Such problems require a knowledge of the ratios between power, speed and the boat. In the present state of our information on this subject, such relation cannot be accurately expressed by any ordinary formula. Several approximate formulas have, however, been employed in the solution of the problem, the best known of which is perhaps the admiralty coefficient formula, in which

H = i.h.p. (indicated horse-power),
D = displacement tons,
V = speed in knots,
C = a coefficient.

The secret in the use of this formula is in the proper selection of the value of the coefficient C, and this can only be done by experience in the way of accurate data concerning the performance of boats of similar size and type. The tendency is to place a too high value on the coefficient, which will of course reduce the estimated i.h.p. with the result that the speed desired will not be obtained and the blame perhaps laid at the door of the engine builders, claiming that the engine does not deliver its rated h.p. when the fault of not obtaining the speed desired would lie somewhere else. At the same time a too low value will increase the i.h.p. beyond that actually required to drive the boat at a given speed. The value

of the coefficient for small yacht work, excluding the racing craft, may be said to rest between 100 and 150.

It will be seen that the resistance, or V in the formula, increases as the cube of the speed, while D, the displacement, is taken at its 2-3 power. Then in order to solve for horse-power we have

$$H = \frac{D^{\frac{2}{3}}\ V^3}{C}.$$

Suppose a boat had a displacement of 6 tons and you desired to drive her 8 knots an hour, the next problem would be the value of C. If of an ordinary cruising type it would be safe to use 120; then we have

$$H = \frac{6^{\frac{2}{3}} \times 8^3}{120} = \frac{3.3 \times 512}{120} = \frac{1689.6}{120}\ 14+ \text{ h.p.}$$

Required the speed of the same boat, other factors being known, we have

$$V = \sqrt[3]{\frac{H\ C}{D^{\frac{2}{3}}}} =$$

$$V \sqrt[3]{\frac{14 \times 120}{3.3}} = \frac{1680}{3.3} = \sqrt[3]{509.} = 7.98 \text{ knots.}$$

Required the value of C, other factors being known, we have

$$C = \frac{D^{\frac{2}{3}}\ V^3}{H} = \frac{3.3 \times 512}{14} = \frac{1689.6}{14} = 120, \text{ value of C.}$$

(The slight difference in the figures of the various problems is due to the fact that the results were not carried far enough beyond the decimal point.)

Under the subject of powering also comes the questions of whether the launch shall be of the single, twin or triple-screw type. There can hardly be any doubt but that a launch will maneuver better with twin or triple screws than would be the case where only one was used, as in turning, one engine could be run ahead while the other was run in the opposite direction, as would be the case with two-stroke engines without clutch, while in the four-stroke engine it would only be necessary to reverse the clutch, in which case a launch could make a turn practically within her length. The same would of course hold good equally well in regard to triple screws, with the additional advantage of being able to run under reduced power when desired by simply shutting off the two side engines or the central one, allowing the propeller in either case to revolve, when underway. This can only be done where there is a clutch attached to the engine or the shaft made to uncouple. The triple-screw arrangement is no doubt the most economical installation that can be put into a launch so far as the consumption of fuel is concerned, as with it one needs only to use the central engine or the two wing engines when cruising, and full power when in a hurry or during a race. The great trouble in a triple-screw arrangement is in the tendency to overpower the yacht, which would result in not securing the speed that should be had with the horse-power. An arrangement of triple screws for a 40-foot launch where 20 h.p. was desired, would call for about a 10-h.p. central engine and 5 h.p. each for the wing engines. There is another objection to both twin and triple-screw arrangements in launches in that they take up too much room and multiply the labor in keeping them in shape while the actual results, so far as speed is concerned, are not so satisfactory as with the single screw. Large ocean steamers do not use twin screws to increase their speed but use them because of the mechanical difficulties of transmitting such enormous power, as they have, through a single shaft.

Another objection to the twin and triple-screw arrangement in small launches is that if one wishes to be secure from total disablement it is necessary to have separate tanks and piping for each engine. This is expensive to install, and at the same time a place for three tanks is not always to be had on small launches without sacrificing some part of the boat that may be wanted for other purposes.

Trial Trip

It is essential for a designer to obtain all the information possible regarding the speed of the boats in order to properly estimate the performances of any new designs, and in order to do so the speed trials should be conducted in a proper manner. The best method is to have two marks exactly a mile apart and to make not less than four runs over the course, noting the time of each run both with and against the tide.

Suppose four runs are made as suggested and you desire to obtain an average. The way to do so is as follows:

North, 7.22 6.66 6.675
South, 6.10 6.69   6.685 speed in miles per hour.
North, 7.28 6.69 6.695
South, 6.12 6.70

It is sometimes customary to average up the four speeds without averaging each pair, which in this case would give a speed of 6.68 as against 6.685, a difference of only .005, surely close enough for the average and just as likely to be correct.

Tools and Instruments

When it comes to the actual work of laying down a design, a certain number of tools and instruments are required, among them being a drawing board. This may be from five to six feet long, and about thirty inches wide will be plenty wide enough. It should be of perfectly clear white pine made up of three or four pieces with the edges doweled, glued and secured on the bottom by three white pine cleats about ⅞ x 4 inches. The top should be planed smooth, sandpapered, and may be varnished or not as desired. A straight edge the same length as the board is also desirable and the best are made of steel, although somewhat more expensive than a wooden one. Two triangles will be found sufficient, one being about 16 inches and the other 6 or 8 inches; they may be either 45 or 60°, the latter being perhaps the one more often used. Triangles are made of wood, hard rubber and celluloid, the latter being by far the best, as they are transparent and consequently enable you to see all of your work. The drawing instruments, such as pen, dividers, etc., are the same as used by architects and engineers and can be bought in regular sets.

In order to draw the curved lines, you will require long, thin pieces of wood known as battens. The best are made of lancewood, but as it is very scarce in this country they are generally made of white pine, hard rubber and celluloid, the latter being very easy to bend and consequently used where the curves are very abrupt or sharp, such as the after ends of water-lines. A hard rubber batten is a little stiffer than a celluloid one and on a cold day should be warmed a little before being used, as they are quite brittle. It is not possible to give the exact sizes required as they vary so, depending on the class of work to be done. For a sheer batten one might be ¼ inch thick by 3-16 inch wide at one end and tapered to 3-32 inch at the other, and say 36 to 40 inches long; two or three straight battens of various sizes would

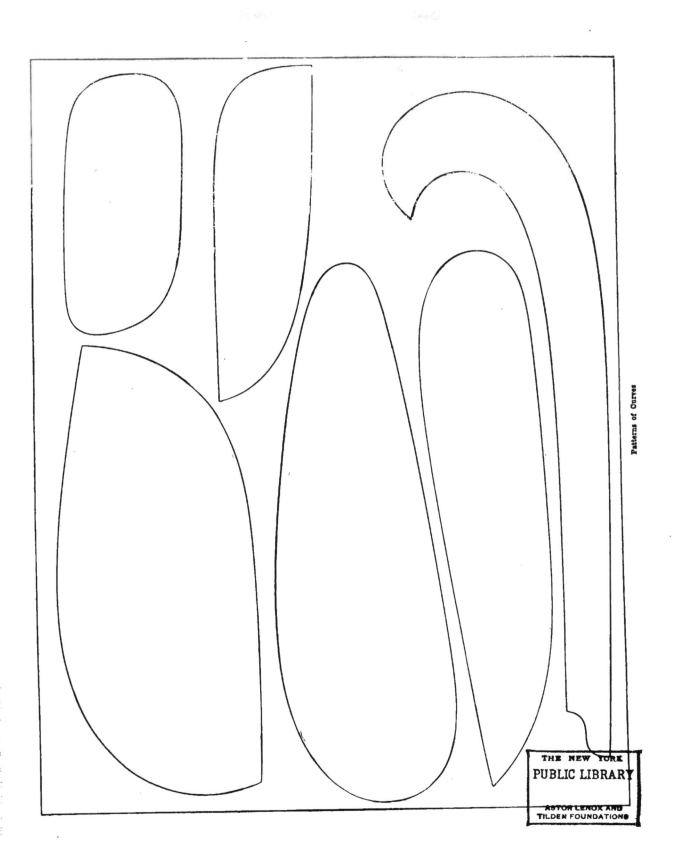

Patterns of Curves

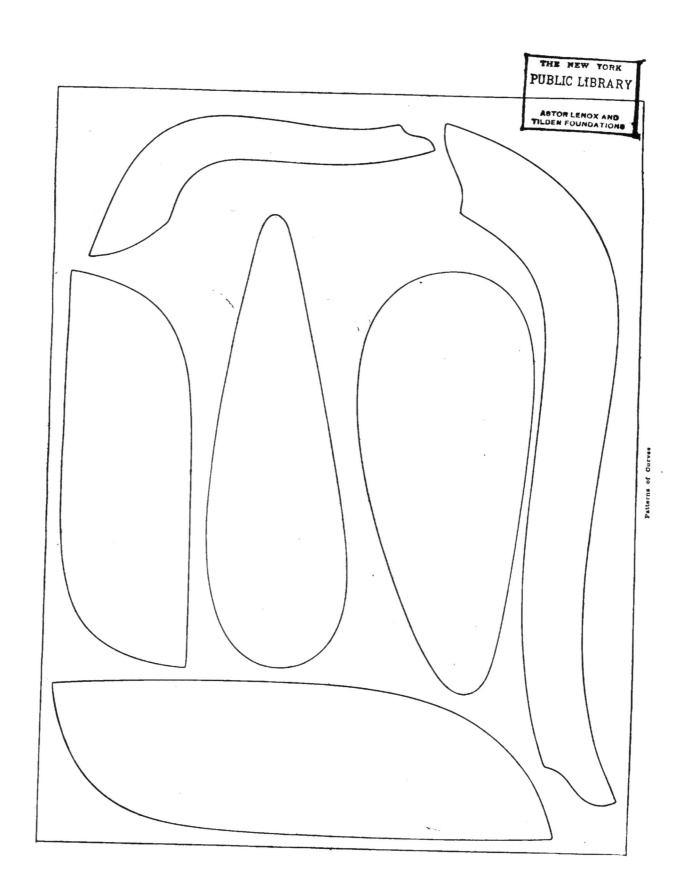

Patterns of Curves

also come in handy and some very small and thin ones for the body plan, as it is much easier to fair up a design when the body plan is drawn in by using battens than when curves are used.

In order to hold the battens in place some sort of weights, known as batten weights, are necessary. These are usually made of lead with pieces of felt glued on the bottom to protect the paper and fitted with little short pieces of wire at one end, known as fingers, which is placed on the batten and holds it in place while the line is being drawn.

In addition a set of curves will be found very useful. These are known as Copenhagen ship curves, and on pp. 19 and 21 will be found some of the most useful. These shapes can be transferred to a piece of ⅛-inch white holly and cut out, the edges being finished off with a coarse file and, say, two grades of sandpaper glued to small pieces of wood, after which the flat sides of the curves may be sandpapered smooth and then filled with oil and rubbed down. This will protect the wood from absorbing ink and they will always remain bright.

The necessary paper to do the drawing on can be either white or cream color; it comes in rolls and can be had any width or length, and is secured and held in place on the drawing board by thumb-tacks.

A planimeter is an instrument used for measuring the areas of irregular figures and by architects to measure the areas of the immersed cross section of a yacht thereby reducing to a considerable extent the calculation necessary in a design. This, while not really needful, is a great help where one has considerable work on hand and time means money. In addition to the foregoing it will be well to have some scales of the following sizes, viz.: ¼, ⅜, ½, ¾, 1, 1½ and 3 inches to the foot.

DESIGN

The first step usual in the design of a power boat is in the getting out of the plan known as the outboard profile of the boat. This is supposed to show the boat, above the L. W. L. or load water-line, as she will appear in the finished condition afloat, with everything on her, such as flags, awning, etc., and for a boat of, say, 32 feet long should be on ½-inch scale, so that the eye can take in the whole boat at once.

The elements that enter into the make-up of a yacht are to a certain extent governed by the ideas and tastes of the architect, as, for instance, the freeboard and sheer. Should a launch of the ordinary hunting cabin,

or raised deck, type be desired, the first thing to be considered is how much freeboard to give her at the bow, stern, and how much the least freeboard should be, taking into consideration where the boat is to be used and the conditions that she would be likely to meet. In cases where a boat is designed for use on large bodies of water, such as Long Island Sound and the Great Lakes, she should possess plenty of freeboard, while if for use on small inland lakes or rivers, the freeboard need not be so great but still possess as ample seaworthiness for the work intended. The form of the sheer is also a matter of taste and it is this that regulates the position of the lowest point of the sheer, some preferring it nearly amidship, while others make it at the extreme after end of the boat and carry it forward to a little beyond the after end of the L. W. L., while still others prefer it at about three-fourths to seven-eighths the length of the yacht from the bow. This, I think, makes by far the best looking sheer that it is possible to put on a yacht. The chief objection to the first sheer is that you do not get enough freeboard at one-fourth the distance from the bow, or if you increase the sheer to obtain this height, you have a bow too high for the rest of the boat; while the second sheer is a very hard one to obtain and keep the boat from having the appearance of a sag at the stern.

Having decided on the sheer, it is necessary to draw in the bow and stern to suit and then the house, bearing in mind the amount of headroom desired, and remember it is not an easy thing to get 6 feet in a 32-foot launch and not have her look top-heavy.

About the right amount of freeboard for a launch of this size, if she is to be used on Long Island Sound, would be 4 feet 5 inches at the bow with a least freeboard of 2 feet 4 inches, and at the stern 2 feet 8 inches.

It is customary before proceeding further to decide on the displacement of your launch which, in this case, as the boat will be heavily built and equipped with a heavy-weight slow-speed engine with ample tank capacity so as to secure good cruising radius, will be, say, 9,200 lb. It is now necessary to decide on a suitable prismatic coefficient of, say, .56, which, on the water-line length decided upon, would give us a midship section area of 9.18 square feet, as follows, using the formula previously explained (see page 9):

$$A = \frac{D}{L\,P} = \frac{144}{15.68} = 9.18 \text{ sq. ft., area of M. S.}$$

The position of the M. S. must be decided either by data gained by actual practice or by that gathered from successful boats of the type being considered, or as near that type as possible. Its position, however, in successful launches of this type may be said to lie from .50 to .60 per cent from the forward end of the water-line

The paper used for getting out the lines should be stretched as tight as possible and held in place at the four corners by thumb-tacks. In laying down a design, it is the usual practice to place the bow to the right and the stern to the left, the half-breadth plan at the bottom of the paper, the sheer plan at the top and the body plan either over the sheer or to one side, it

nine inches apart, if your drawing is to be one inch to the foot, which is about right for a boat of this size. From the first line drawn there should be erected perpendiculars every two or three feet apart extending far enough above the load water-line to take the sheer line, which in this case would be about five feet. Parallel to and about twelve inches out from the first line drawn there should be drawn in two additional lines, which are known as buttock lines. These show the form of the boat if she were cut lengthwise and a little off the center. The load water-line shows the shape of the boat if sawed through at that point, or should the boat be at rest in water, the water freeze, and the boat be

Mary Anna. Dimensions—Length O. A. 68 Ft., Length W. L. 60 Ft., Breadth 23 Ft., Draught 4 Ft.

being a matter of taste with the designer. Along the lower edge of the paper a line should be drawn which will be used to represent the center of the yacht, while above it and a little more than the half-breadth of the boat there should be another line drawn parallel to it, which is known as the base line; a little above this is drawn another line parallel to it at a slightly further distance than the draught of the boat. This line is known as the load water-line, while above and below it should be drawn additional water-lines to assist in fairing the boat up. These are generally about six or

lifted out the shape of the load water-line would exactly correspond to the shape of the upper edge of the ice. The cross sections show the shape the boat would be if cut through at any one of the various sections.

In drawing the sections, or body plan as it is called, you will always find the sections from amidship forward on one side of the center line and from amidship aft on the opposite side. The forebody being on the right-hand side if the bow is to the right, or on the left-hand side if the bow is to the left.

The sheer is now transferred from the outboard pro-

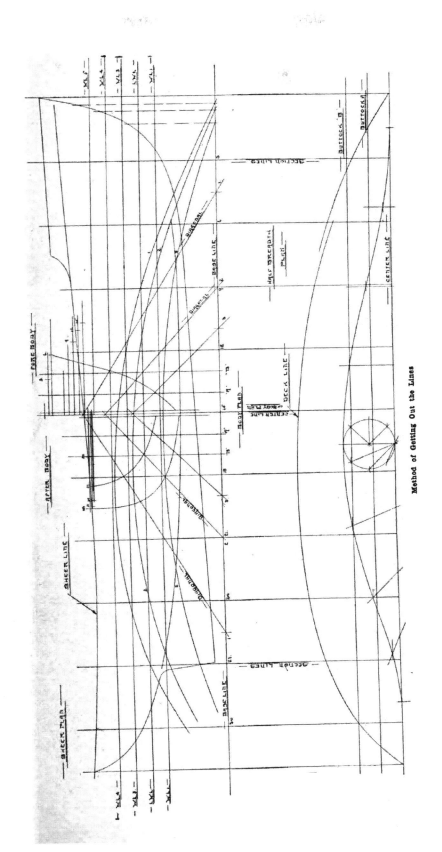

Method of Getting Out the Lines

file to the paper you will get the lines out on and the bow and stern drawn in. Having decided on a displacement, area of midship section and position of same, a curve of areas, consisting of a curve of versed sine for the forebody and a trochoid for the after-body, should be drawn in to act as a guide, the position from which the curves are drawn being the position of the midship section previously decided upon.

The underwater body is now sketched in and also the deck line on the half-breadth plan, after which the M. S. (midship section) can be sketched in until its shape is satisfactory and the area corresponds with that shown in the M. S. on the curve of areas.

A section at four or six feet from the bow and stern may be sketched in and a diagonal line drawn through the three spots formed by the intersection of the distance, measured along the diagonal line in the body plan, to the three sections, and this distance laid off from the base line on each section line as shown. This operation may now be reversed for the balance of the sections not yet drawn in and the position of their intersection laid off on the diagonal line in the body plan and then the sections sketched in after the intersection of the various sections has been laid off on the line representing the half siding of keel and the intersection at the deck and sheer lines.

These points may not be such as to give one a fair line, so it is necessary to come and go on the various sections until all the points correspond with each other. After the first diagonal is drawn in, two or three more may be drawn to assist in fairing up. Diagonals are used in fairing up a boat in preference to water-lines and buttocks, as the line crosses the sections in the body plan at nearer right angles, so that any unfairing is more readily seen and corrected. The various sections must not only be faired up with relation to each other, but the area in that part below the L. W. L. must be made such that the displacement will come out as decided upon with the given coefficient, and the center of buoyancy must also be kept in its proper fore-and-aft position.

When this part of the work is done and the boat fair, the various water-lines and buttocks may be drawn in, and the title added, when this part of the design may be considered finished.

The other drawings, such as cabin, construction, midship section and details, can be taken up in the order in which you may desire. The cabin layout is, of course, a matter of purely personal taste and any amount of time and thought can be spent on it. The construction drawings are sometimes made a part of the cabin plan and with the midship section, giving the size of all members going into the boat, show the method to be followed in building the launch. The offsets are to enable the builder to lay the boat down to full size and are put down in feet, inches and eighths of an inch.

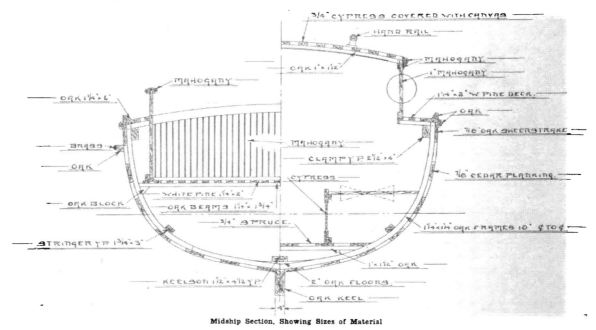

Midship Section, Showing Sizes of Material

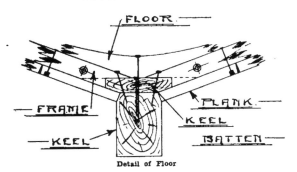

Detail of Floor

The half-breadths being taken down from the center line and all heights taken from the base line. The diagonals are taken along the diagonal from its intersection with the center line of the body plan.

CONSTRUCTION

The construction adopted in the average cruising launch of under forty feet varies but little and that to a great extent by the form of the launch and the material

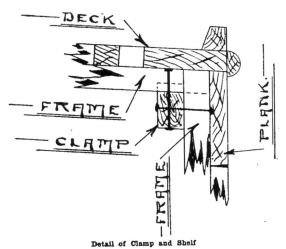

Detail of Clamp and Shelf

at hand for her construction. The best woods for the construction of boats in this part of the country are oak for the keel, stem, stern timber, frames and dead-wood, where it is possible to get it in the sizes required; yellow pine may be used for dead-wood, but this is not

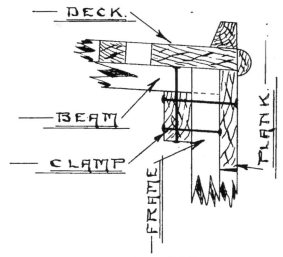

Detail of Clamp and Shelf

nearly so good as oak for the other parts. The stem and stern timbers are frequently made of hackmatack, and it is very satisfactory for this purpose and also for knees and breasthooks, although I have frequently seen knees and breasthooks made of Jersey cedar that proved equally as good, and in some quarters much more readily obtained. The frame is usually made of oak, steam-bent, although where elm can be obtained it is much better, as it is easily bent and very tough. The frames, as a rule, come down on top of the keel and meet the corresponding frame, on the opposite side, at the center, the heel of the frames being secured to the keel by a long nail or screw. In this case it is customary to put an oak block on top of the keel, between each pair of frames, and extending out on each side of the keel far enough to form a back rabbet to the garboard and to make a landing edge for the garboard to be fastened to. Another method is to fasten on top of the keel an oak plank one inch thick and two or three inches wider than the keel, sometimes known as a covering board, and land the heel of the frames on this either by cutting them to fit the garboard or by letting them lap over the covering board, filling in the space between

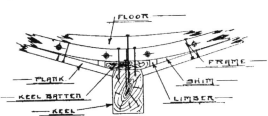

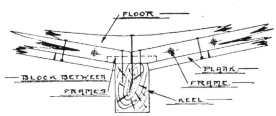

Details of Keel and Floors

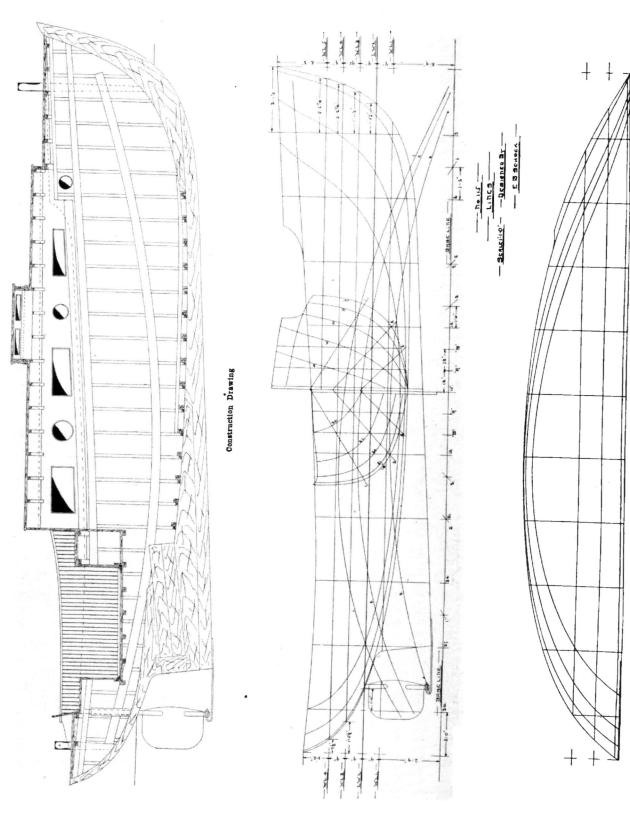

Construction Drawing

Hull
Scantlings

Lines
Designed By
E. B. Schock

Base Line

Base Line

Lines of Thirty-Two-Foot Cruiser. Complete

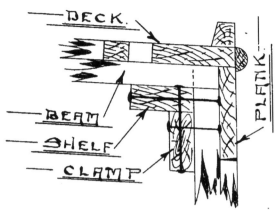

Detail of Clamp and Shelf

ing. Stringers, where wide enough to have two fastenings in each frame, should have one through the frame and the other through the frame and plank; but where not wide enough to have two, one through the frame will be sufficient. The clamp should be secured in the same way as the stringer, if wide enough for two fastenings; but if only wide enough for one there should be a fastening through the frame and plank in every other frame. The shelf is sometimes made separate from the clamp and sometimes a part of it, in which case the clamp must of course be somewhat larger. Where it is made separate it should be fastened through the clamp. The clamp and shelf should in either case be secured to a breasthook at each end.

Keelsons are usually made of yellow pine although oak is sometimes used. They are placed on top of the floors and fastened with pieces of iron or brass rods cut so as to extend down through the floors and some distance into the keel, thus tying the three members securely together.

Limber holes, always a cause of trouble, can be made by cutting out a piece of the frame and floor about two inches from the keel, care being taken not to make the limber so large as to weaken the frame and floor. Where a shim is used the end next to the covering board may be cut away for a distance of an inch to form a limber. This makes the best kind of a limber and is a strong recommendation for this kind of construction.

The planking usually used on a small launch is cedar, although yellow pine is sometimes used and once in a while oak for garboards or far below water. Mahogany is also used where a highly finished hull is desired. The cedar should be as clear as possible while the knots should be tight, and the planks should have the bark

the garboard and the frame with a tapered piece of pine or cedar, known as a shim. This will allow the garboard to be fitted and properly fastened without showing a hollow that is often seen in the garboards of boats built in this manner. The heel of the frames being secured to the keel the same in either case.

Floors are usually made of oak, although hackmatack or apple knees make excellent ones, especially up around the bow where the boat is sharp. These should be secured to the keel where no keelson is used with a long nail or by iron or brass rods cut to the required length, bored for and driven over rings. They should also be secured to the frames, riveted through fastenings being the best.

Yellow pine, Oregon pine or spruce is the wood generally used for clamps, shelf or stringer, and should be in as long lengths as is possible to secure it. It is, however, impossible to always secure it in full lengths and consequently a scarf must be made. This should be plenty long and securely fastened by through rivet-

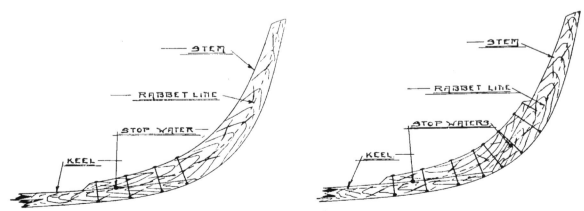

Details of Stem

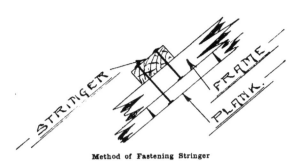

Method of Fastening Stringer

on its edges in order to have it as wide as possible. In selecting yellow pine, see that it is free from sap and rosin. The oak used for garboards and sheer-strakes is, as a rule, fairly well seasoned when it reaches here, as it is almost always what is known as Western oak, all the Eastern oak suitable for planking having apparently been used up long ago. Planks are put on or secured in various ways, being either nailed, riveted or screw fastened. In a nailed plank the nails sometimes extend through the frames and are clinched, while where the frame is heavy enough they merely extend about three-fourths the way through the frame. In either case, it is customary to bore for the fastening before being driven. In copper riveting the nails extend through the frame about one-quarter of an inch, the burr is then put on, the point cut off close up to the burr and the end riveted up, having a person on the outside of the boat holding on the head of the nail a piece of iron or small sledge-hammer to prevent its backing out. Screw fastening has the advantage of requiring only one person to put them in, but the disadvantage of cutting away more of the frame, which is only a disadvantage in a boat having a very light frame. The plank ends are, as a rule, secured with brass screws, although galvanized nails are sometimes used. Butts should come between frame and be secured to an oak block the same width as the plank and about the depth of the frames.

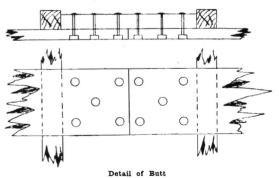

Detail of Butt

The best method of fastening is with copper rivets, having about five in the ends of each plank. In yacht work it is customary to countersink the heads of all fastenings in the plank and fill the hole with a wooden plug, after first painting the hole with white lead to make the plug stay in place. Where this is not done, the heads of the nails are usually puttied.

Deck beams are usually made of oak although yellow pine is sometimes used. They are generally cut to shape, as they would not keep their shape if bent as the crown is so small. Extra heavy beams are placed at any openings in the deck, and at such places as the end of cockpits and each end of house. The ends of the beams are sometimes dovetailed into the clamp, but where a shelf is fitted they are usually fastened through the shelf without dovetail. Where the beams are cut short, as in the way of the house, the best method is to dovetail them, as it makes a much better job besides being so much neater in the cabin. This is also much better where the house is to be built up with a staving having a thin finishing piece on the inside and out.

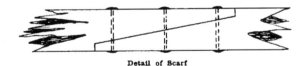

Detail of Scarf

There is no wood better than white pine for decks. It is usually laid in narrow strips sometimes parallel to the plank-sheer and sometimes parallel to the center line of the boat. When laid parallel to the center line of the boat it is notched into the plank-sheer in order to do away with the sharp point which could not be properly fastened. The planks are secured to the beams by nails countersunk and plugged, and are sometimes edge fastened in addition. Plank-sheer are made of either oak or mahogany secured in the same manner as the deck, while the butts are usually made to take in two or three beams. The plank-sheer in addition to being fastened to the beams is sometimes fastened to the sheer-strake.

Cockpits in launches are built, as a rule, with a slope aft in order that they will drain properly when underway, as the action of the screw tends to draw the water out of them. It has been noticed, however, in running before a heavy sea that the water will sometimes be forced through the scupper and into the cockpit, notwithstanding the action of the propeller. This may be avoided by keeping the cockpit as high as possible. The

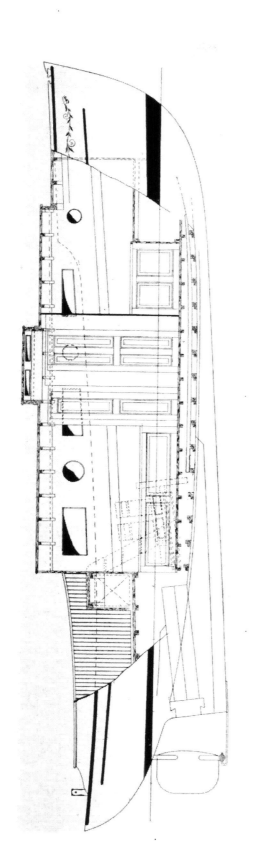

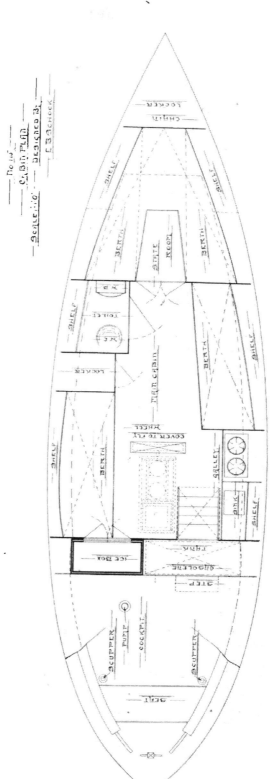

Cabin Plan of Thirty-Two-Foot Cruiser

Nomad II. Dimensions—Length O. A. 36 Ft., Length W. L. 32.10 Ft., Breadth 9.6 Ft., Draught 2.8 Ft.

height of the cockpit is also regulated to a certain extent by the height of the house that the helmsman must see over. This height may roughly be fixed at 42 inches, that being about as high as it is possible to have the house above the cockpit floor. The floor of the cockpit is constructed in much the same manner as the deck, the beams being spaced usually one to each frame, and either secured to the frames with a block under the end of the beam or supported on a fore-and-aft member known as a rising. The sill to which the staving is fastened should be of white pine or some other wood that is easily worked and should be rabbeted into the

floor about one-quarter of an inch, set in white lead and screwed fast. The staving usually rests on this sill and is secured to it and also to the inner end of the deck beams. Sometimes the staving runs down to the floor and is held in place by a locking piece and faced off with a quarter-round. This, however, does not make nearly so good a job although somewhat cheaper.

Within a short space of time the houses on cruising launches have undergone radical changes, the most pronounced of which is no doubt that of the raised deck type, where the sides of the boat are carried up to form the house. This is by far the simplest method of con-

Twenty-Two-Foot Launch Campbell

Launching a Cruiser

structing a house and also the easiest one to make tight, as the sides of it are treated in the same manner as the sides of the boat, being as it is a part of the same. The roof in all cases being covered with canvas turned down over the sides and having the edges covered with a half-round. Where the boat has a deck along the sides of the house, it is of course necessary to build the house as it were separate. Houses of this nature are made of one piece of plank, if not too long or too wide, placed on top of the deck and bolted fast, mahogany being the best wood for the purpose, as it gives a good finish. Where it is desired to build the house up with a staving and finishing pieces, the staving is usually tongue-and-grooved spruce and is first secured to the end of

Annaweta. Designed and Built by Fred S. Nock. Length O. A. 57 Ft, Length W. L. 51 Ft., Breadth 12.6 Ft., Draught 4 Ft.

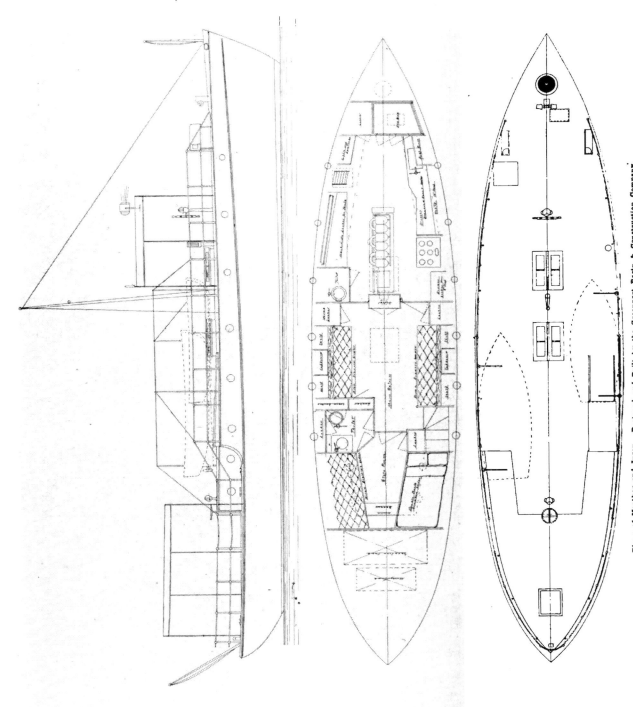

Plans of Heather and Iwana. Designed and Built by the Greenport Basin & Construction Company

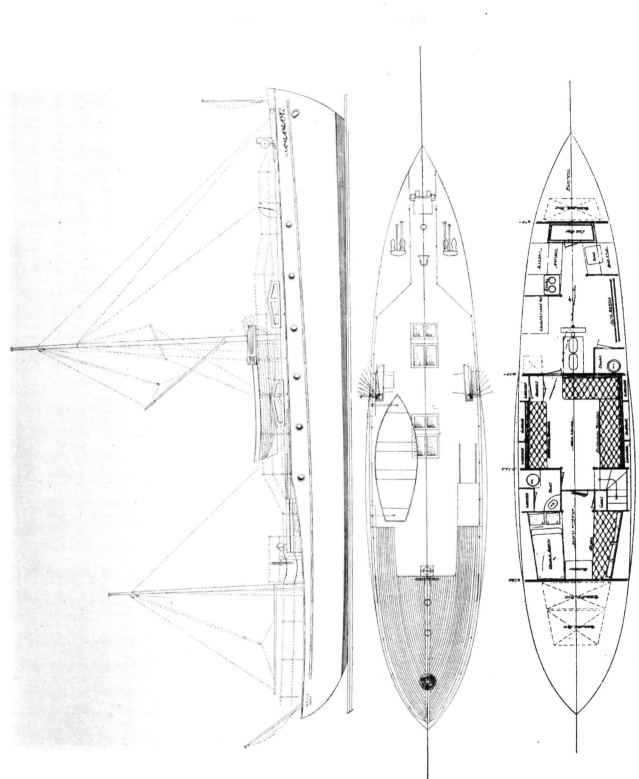

Plans of Nereides II. Designed by Whittelsey & Whitaker and Built by the Stamford Motor Company

Spanish Fishing Boat, Built by Thornycroft

Power Lifeboat Attached to the Cape May Station

Viator. Dimensions—Length O. A. 90 Ft., Length W. L. 85 Ft., Breadth 14.6 Ft., Draught 6 Ft.

the deck beams, the finishing pieces, or wrappers as they are sometimes called, being put on later. This method has the advantage of being able to have a mahogany house on the outside and a white pine one on the inside, as some do not prefer to have a mahogany cabin owing to it being so dark. The roof of the cabin in all cases is practically the same, consisting of oak beams and pine roof covered with canvas. The canvas should always be stretched on dry and laid in white lead. The edges should be turned down and securely fastened with copper tacks, copper being used, as any other kind will rust in time and streak the sides of the cabin, and finished off with a half-round of the same material as the

sides of the house. Where skylights or hatches are used on top of the cabin, it is best to cut the canvas with an inch to turn up on the inside of the skylight, and finish it off with a half-inch strip of mahogany or whatever wood the skylight is made of, or you will have trouble from the skylight leaking. The same, of course, applies to hatches. The best material for skylights, hatches and other deck fittings is teak and mahogany; the first is hard to get in this country and costs about twice what mahogany does, so that it is seldom used on small boats. The other fittings, such as windlass, bitts, cleats, chocks, etc., are a matter of taste with the owner or designer.

Cigarette. Dimensions—Length O. A. 121.10 Ft., Length W. L. 117 Ft., Breadth 14.6 Ft., Draught 4.6 Ft.

Zingaree. Dimensions—Length O. A. 81 Ft., Length W. L. 72 Ft., Breadth 10.7 Ft., Draught 3.5 Ft.

Tramp. Dimensions—Length O. A. 82 Ft., Length W. L. 72 Ft., Breadth 10.9 Ft., Draught 2.7 Ft.

Shada. Dimensions—Length O. A. 96 Ft., Length W. L. 84 Ft., Breadth 15.7 Ft., Draught 5 Ft.

Fifty-Foot Cruiser, Ruth

Small launches are usually calked with cotton and the seams filled with a mixture of putty and white lead while the decks are almost always payed with a seam preparation. The rudder and rudder fittings below water should always be of brass or bronze, as otherwise galvanic action will set up between the rudder and propeller. This does not apply to boats used in fresh water. Where a boat is supplied with a fender or rubbing strip and stem-board, it should always be of brass, as a galvanized iron one will rust, and the sides of the boat always show the rust-stains under every fastening.

CYGNET

This boat was built from designs of F. K. Lord, for H. Edwards-Ficken, of Huntington, N. Y., the requirements of the design being a craft which could be used in safety and comfort as an afternoon family runabout on Huntington Bay and adjacent waters. She is 28 feet over all, 5 feet breadth, and draws 22 inches. The construction is substantial and rather heavy for a craft of this type.

The keel is 1¾ by 5½ inches, frames ¾ inch square, with floors on every frame and extra heavy ones in wake of engine beds, which extend well forward and aft and give great strength to hull of boat. The cockpit and decks are finished in mahogany and the best of materials was used throughout.

The engine is a 15-h.p. Ferro, which drives the craft 9½ miles per hour. The engine is not being run at its maximum revolutions, but at top speed the craft should do 12 miles per hour.

Fast Open Runabout, Trente Sept

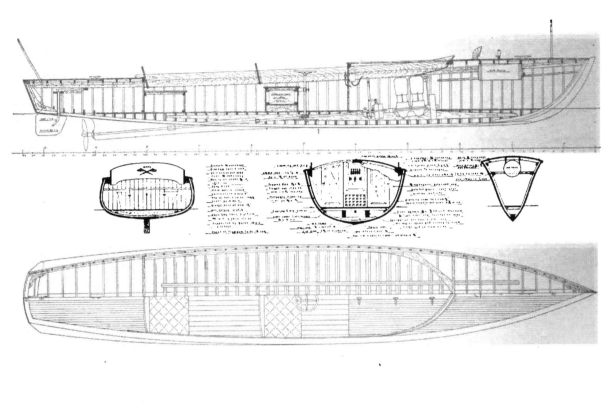

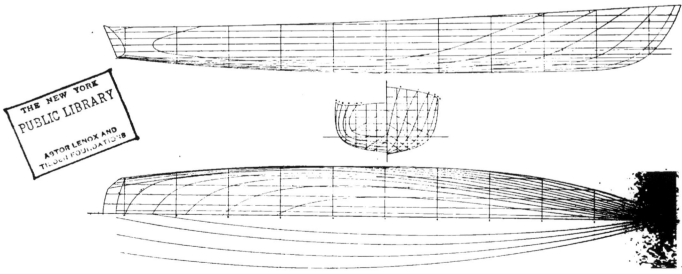

Twenty-Eight Footer.   Designed by Fred K. Lord

Ngaru. Forty-Two-Foot New Zealand Cruiser

Sixty-Foot Great Lakes Cruiser Marguerite

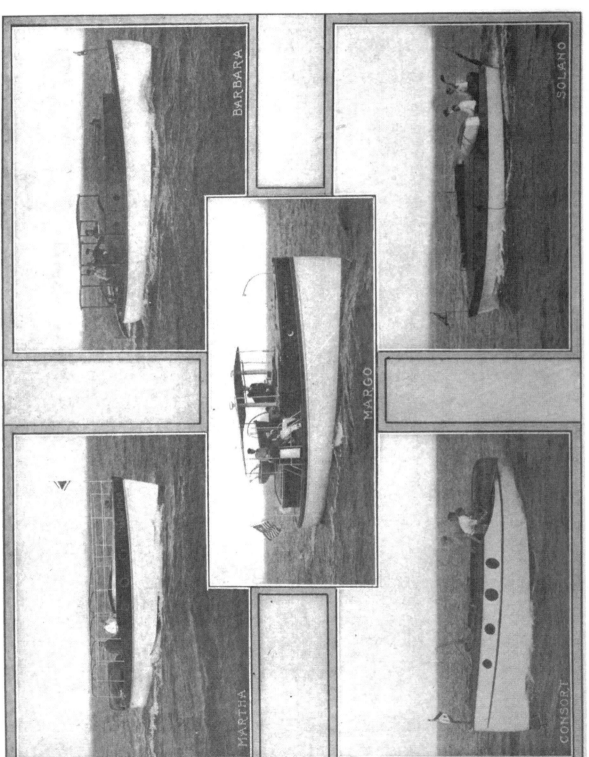

Contestants in the 1908 Block Island Race

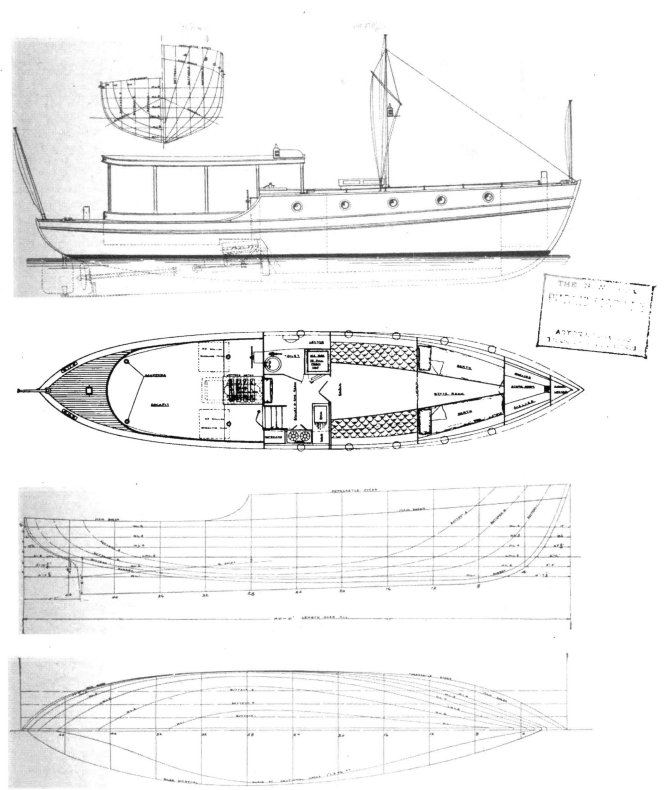

Arcady. 40 Ft. O. A. Designed by Stuart B. Kingsbury, Manitowoc, Wis.

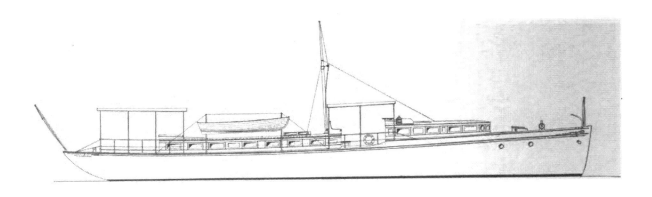

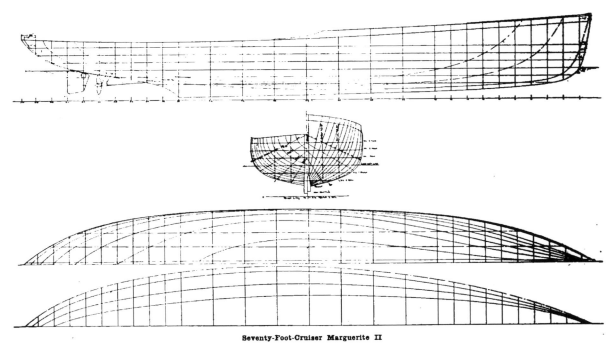

Seventy-Foot-Cruiser Marguerite II

Dimensions—Length O. A. 71 Ft., Length W. L. 63.3 Ft., Breadth 14 Ft., Draught 3.8 Ft.

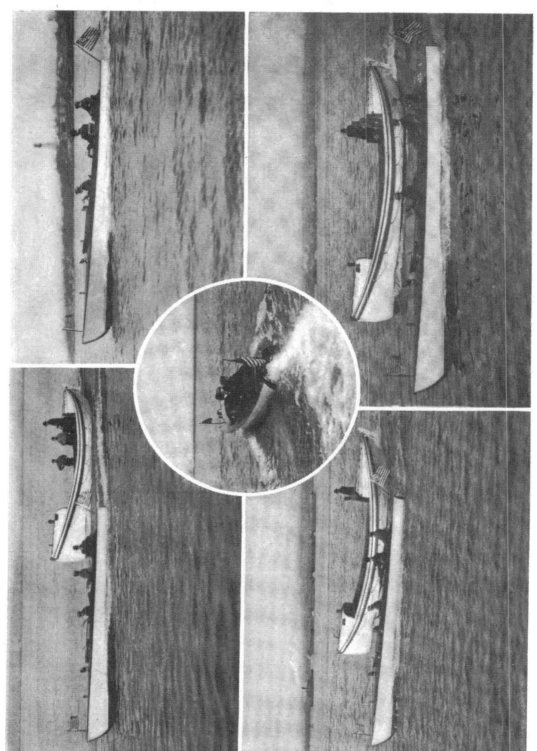

United States Government Lifeboats, and Special Boats

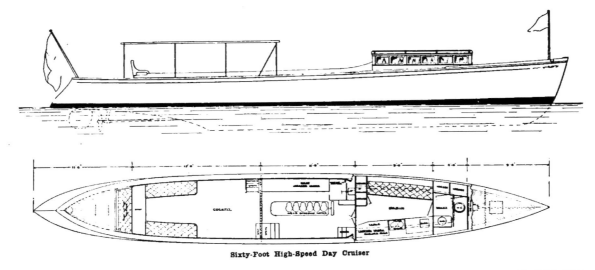

Sixty-Foot High-Speed Day Cruiser

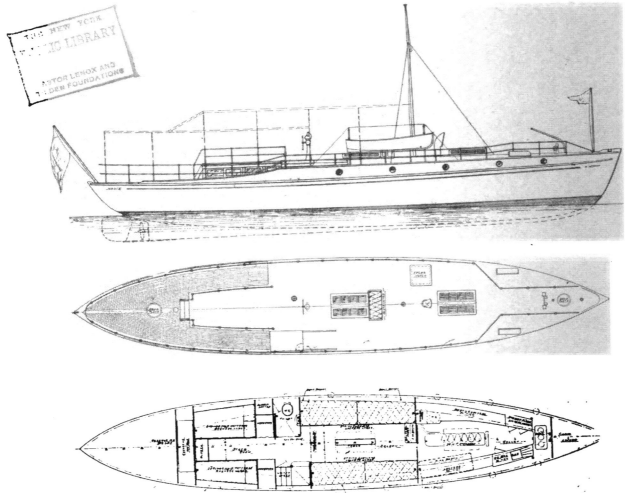

Sixty-Foot Cruiser

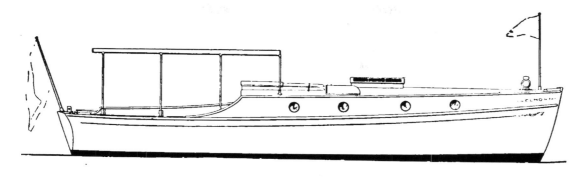

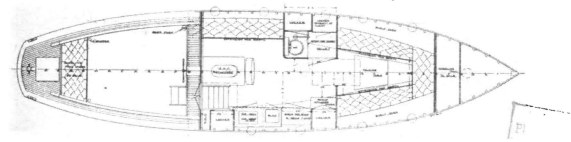

Thirty-Four-Footer, Designed by H. W. Patterson, New York City

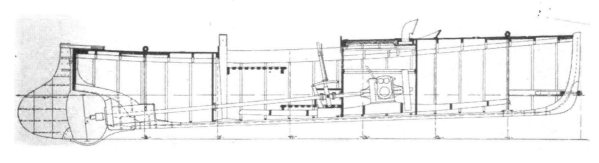

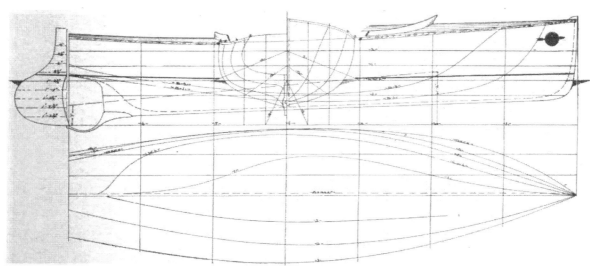

Fourteen-Foot Power Tender

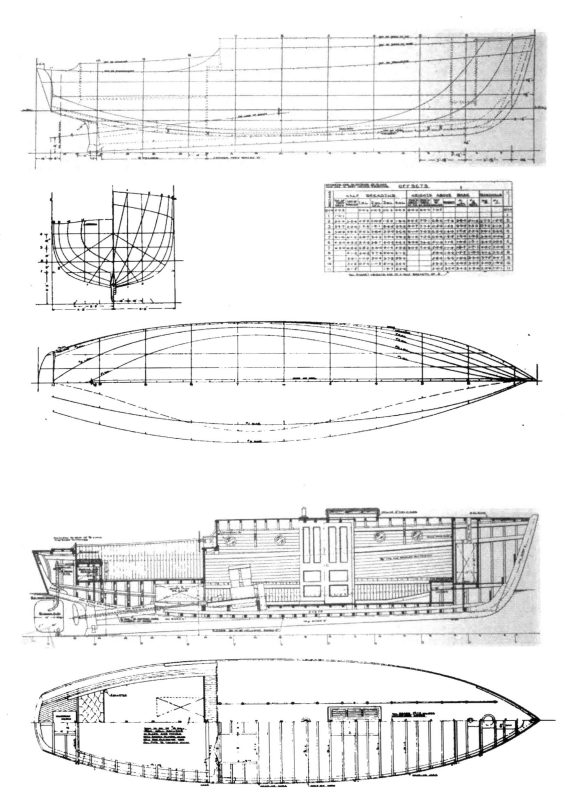

Lines and Construction Plans of Thirty-Four-Footer

A Twenty-Foot Power Cruiser

Designed for use as a week-end cruiser on the Potomac River, Clam would be a suitable boat for most any small body of water and one in which a couple of fellows could knock about to their hearts' content.

For the most part of simple construction, the boat could be easily built by an amateur, at a cost of $150 or thereabouts for the hull. As will be seen at a glance Clam is a radical departure from the usual type of small cruiser, and, too, as the name will suggest, no attention was paid to speed; just a good-natured little ship to loaf around in Saturday afternoons and Sunday is all that was attempted, and she was made as small as possible and obtain any sleeping accommodations at all.

As to dimensions she is something like this:

Length o. a.	20 feet 0	inches
Length w. l.	19 " 0	"
Breadth, extreme ...	5 " 8	"
Breadth, w. l.	4 " 11	"
Draught, extreme ...	1 " 11	"
Freeboard, bow	3 " 0	"
Freeboard, stern	2 " 5⅝	"
Freeboard, least	1 " 11⅜	"

To build this boat the first requisite, of course, is a suitable place, and tools.

For laying down, which will be a simple operation, a smooth floor or large sheet of paper will be necessary.

The base line and load water-line are first struck in—2 feet apart—and the stations set up perpendicular to them at intervals of 2 feet.

All dimensions necessary will be found either on the table of offsets or the keel plan. The lines are to outside of planking, of course, which is ¾ inch thick, so the moulds must be that much less all around than given by the lines. The moulds may be of any ¾ or ⅞-inch stuff which will answer the purpose. When making these, measure 1½ inches each way from the chime, connect the two points and saw off the mould along this line. This is to take the chime log.

The stem of hackmatack or oak and the keel, shaft log, and stern timber of oak are all sided 3 inches and moulded as shown on the keel plan; all securely fastened together with ¼ or 5-16-inch galvanized iron bolts.

A hole of size to take the sleeve for a reversing propeller should be carefully bored in shaft log.

The transom is 1-inch oak well cleated all around to take the ends of the planking (cut these cleats at the chime the same as the moulds) and having a heavy oak knee to the stern timber—well bolted.

Set the boat up with the load water-line horizontal either upright on substantial blocking or inverted, in which case the moulds may all be made deeper and be fastened to the floor, making a more substantial form, the easier way to build a small boat.

In the latter case make all the moulds of such a depth that when set up the load water-line will be about 3 feet 6 inches above the floor.

Nail a straight cleat across each mould so that its lower and straight edge will represent the water-line, then you can set your level on this when you are setting up the inverted mould and also stretch a line through to see if the moulds are all at the proper height. See that they are also plumb fore and aft and square with the center line struck on the floor.

Clam, A Twenty-Foot Power Cruiser, Designed by L. M. Thompson

Having fastened the moulds, keel, stem, and transom in position, bend three ribbands around the moulds, one being placed with its lower edge just where the top of the sheer-strake will come, while the other two are respectively about 6 inches above and 6 inches below the chime.

Now put the chime logs in place and cut in the bevel at each mould so that when dressed to a width of about 3 inches on the inside, the edges of the logs will be perpendicular to the sides and bottom of the moulds and thus make a fit with the planking. The remainder of the work on these can be done after the boat is planked, so the logs may be tacked in place after beveling the edges.

The frames may now be put in. These are nailed to

strake may be oak. A little care must be used in fitting the planking, especially on the bottom, and spilings will be necessary, but there need be no serious difficulty. Bear in mind that a space for calking is left on the outside of the seams.

After the planking is all on it should be smoothed up with plane and sandpaper, together with the chime logs, which may be neatly rounded.

The hole should be bored now for the rudder-post sleeve as it cannot well be done from the inside. The sleeve should be of brass or galvanized iron, 1 inch inside diameter, about 6 inches long and threaded to screw into knee and stern timber and to take the stuffing box it must have on its upper end.

Dolphin, Ex-Crosby Cat with 9-H.P. Grant-Ferris Engine, Speed 8 Miles per Hour

the top of the keel, except at the after end, where they are mortised into the shaft log and dead-wood. The ends at the chime are neatly fitted over, and nailed to the logs and an oak knee placed on top, screw-fastened to the end of each section of the frame and having a ¼-inch galvanized through bolt to the chime log, the head being well countersunk in the log, to allow latter to be dressed off later. The upper ends of the frames are tacked to the upper ribband for the present.

The floors come next, of oak, well fastened to the frames and keel. They are 2 inches thick under the engine.

The planking should be cedar or yellow pine, ¾ inch thick, preferably in single lengths, and the sheer-

The calking can be done easily now if the boat is upside down, and a priming coat of paint put on, after which braces are put in and the boat lifted off the moulds, otherwise better leave the calking till she is all done.

The clamps, breast-hook and the knees at the stern transom go in next and then the inside of the hull is given a coat of paint.

The rudder-post sleeve should be put in with its stuffing box setting but a little above the knee through which the sleeve is screwed. No other support will be necessary, as the bottom of the rudder is housed in the shoe.

Now is the time to install the engine, a 4 or 5 h.p., turning about 500 r.p.m. The bed to suit the engine, of about 2-inch oak, should be snugly fitted over the frames and floors and well fastened. Two copper tanks of a capacity of 10 gallons each are shown, with galvanized iron drip-pans having scuppers leading overboard. These pans extend to the deck and are flanged over the beams, making a tight job. Filling plugs in the deck and removable sections of the latter furnish easy access to the tanks.

When the cockpit is arranged, suitable hatches for access to the engine must be provided.

The propeller reverse is under the cabin floor with a rod and lever leading to the reverse lever in the cockpit, which passes through the cockpit floor.

The spark and throttle controls also pass through the floor, to bell-cranks connected to the timer and carbureter. A foot lever is arranged to throw in a simple jaw clutch on the crank-shaft which connects the starting lever and which will be thrown out as soon as the engine starts. If desired the oil cups may also be arranged in the cockpit.

The bulkhead at the forward end of the cockpit has a crown of 12 inches. A heavy carline extends from it to the stem, over which the deck beams may be bent.

The house and after deck beams are sawed to a crown of 4 inches in 5 feet. Decks may be of any light wood, ½ inch thick and covered with canvas.

If a simpler style of cabin is desired, plain tongued-and-grooved staving may be used, and round ports.

The companion steps are removable, giving space for extensions to the transoms, which will make a 6-foot 8-inch berth, plenty long enough for the average fellow, and about 2 feet wide.

There is 4 feet headroom in the cabin as shown.

Glass Cabin Day Cruiser Aliquippa

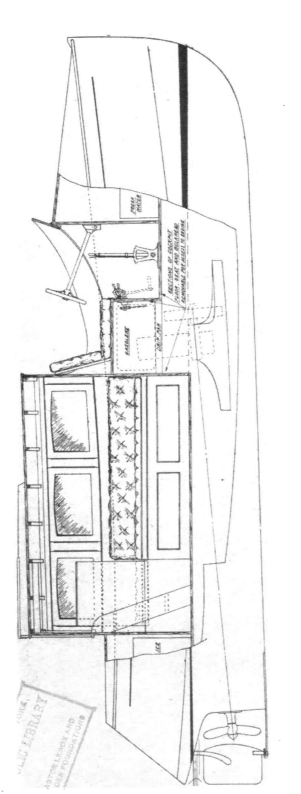

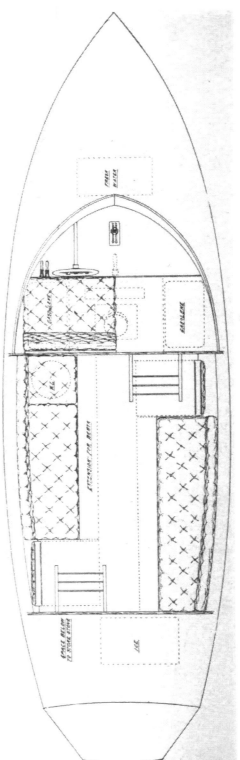

Accommodation Plan of Twenty-Footer Clam

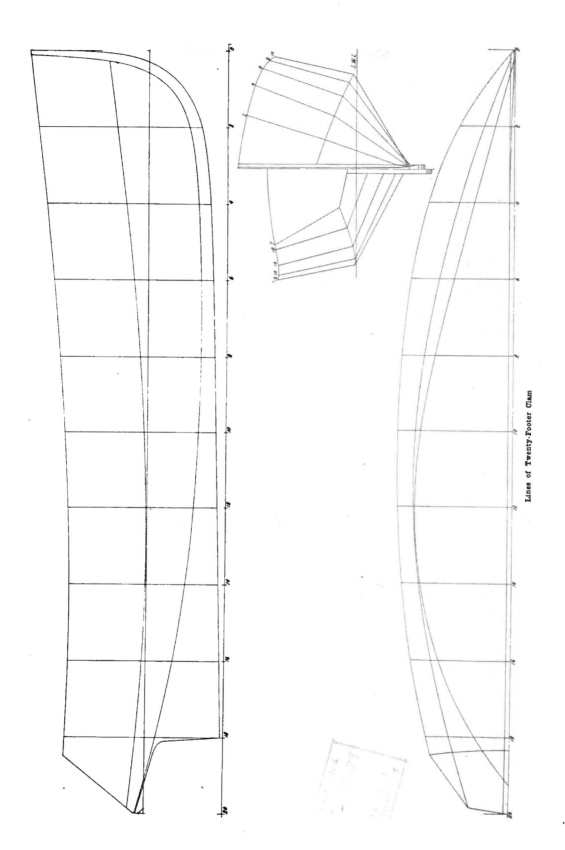

Lines of Twenty-Footer Clam

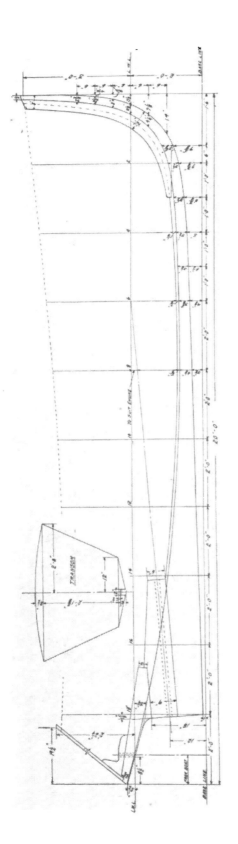

STATION	0	2	4	6	8	10	12	14	16	18	20
				HEIGHTS ABOVE BASE LINE							
SHEER	5-0-0	4-9-2	4-5-6	4-4-1	4-2-5	4-1-1	3-11-7	3-11-3	3-11-4	4-0-3	4-0-6
CHINE	3-0-3	2-9-2	2-6-5	2-4-1	2-2-2	2-1-0	2-0-2	2-0-2	2-1-1	2-2-6	2-8-6
RABBET	-	0-11-3	0-9-9	0-7-6	0-7-5	0-6-3	0-9-6	1-0-2	1-3-6	1-9-6	2-2-3
KEEL	-	0-7-6	0-3-0	0-1-1	0-3-5	0-3-0	0-2-0	0-2-0	0-1-9	0-1-0	-
				HALF BREADTHS							
SHEER	0-0-2	1-4-6	2-2-0	2-7-1	2-9-6	2-11-0	2-11-6	2-10-6	2-6-4	2-1-3	1-0-0
CHINE	-	0-9-0	1-4-5	1-10-9	2-2-7	2-5-4	2-6-0	2-5-4	2-4-2	1-6-9	1-1-4
L.W.L.	-	0-5-5	0-11-7	1-6-0	1-11-5	2-1-4	2-5-9	2-5-6	1-10-0	0-10-5	-

LINES TO OUTSIDE OF PLANK
DIMENSIONS IN FEET, INCHES, AND EIGHTHS

— CLAM —

— OFFSETS-SECTIONS —

SCALE 1 in. 1 ft

Table of Offsets and Scantling Dimensions of Clam

Books for a Nautical Library

ADVANCE IN PRICES—Owing to the increased cost of paper, printing and binding, we are obliged to advance all our new editions of former $1 books to $1.25

BOAT HANDLING, ETC.

RUDDER ON SERIES—

On Flags, Their Origin and Use. By A. F. Aldridge	$0.25
On Navigation Simplified. By McArthur	1.25
Handy Jack Book of Navigation Tables........paper	.75
On Sights. By Sheppard	1.00
On Yacht Sailing	.50
On Yacht Etiquette. By Patterson	1.00
Southward in the Roamer. By H. C. Roome	1.00
Art and Science of Sailmaking. By S. B. Sadler	6.00
Awnings and Tents, Construction and Design. By Ernest Chandler	5.00
Boat-Building and Boating. By Beard	1.35
Boating Book for Boys	1.50
Book of the Motor Boat. By Verrill	1.25
Book of the Sail Boat. By Verrill	1.25
British and Colonial Flags	.60
Handbook of American Yacht Racing Rules	2.00
The Helmsman's Handbook. By B. Heckstall Smith	4.00
Kedge Anchor. By Patterson	1.00
Knots and Splices. By Capt. Jutsum	.75
Knots, Splices and Rope Work. By B. Verrill	1.00
Knots. By A. F. Aldridge	1.00
Know Your Own Ship	3.00
Masting and Rigging. By Robert Kipping	1.25
Motor Boats, Construction and Operation	1.50
Practical Boat Sailing. By Frazar	1.00
Racing Schedule Sheets	.10
Sailing. By Knight	.75
Sailing Ships and Their Story. By E. Keble Chatterton	2.50
Sails and Sailmaking	1.25
Small Boat Sailing. By Knight..............$2.25; by mail	2.50
Small Yacht. By R. A. Boardman..............$2.50; by mail	2.63
The Landsman. By Ensign L. Edson Raff, 1st Bat. Nav. Mil., N. Y.	.50
Yachtsman's Guide 1919 ....$1.00; by mail	1.25
Yacht Sails. By Patterson	1.00

SEAMANSHIP

Fore-and-Aft Seamanship	.50
Merchant Marine Manual	1.00
Modern Seamanship. By Knight..............$3.00; by mail	3.25
Notes on Stowage. C. H. Hillcoat	3.75
Practical Seamanship. Todd & Whall	10.00
Reed's Seamanship	3.00
Seamanship. By Doane	1.25
Tait's New Seamanship. 5th Edition	3.00

SIGNALLING

International Signals—A Few Ways to Use the Code	.25
Nautical Telegraph Code. By D. H. Bernard	1.25
Night Signals of World's Shipping	1.25
Signal Card	.75
Signalling—International Code Signals	1.00
Signal Reminder. By D. H. Bernard	.50

BOATBUILDING

RUDDER HOW TO SERIES—

How to Build and Rig a Cruising Yawl	1.00
How to Build an 18-Foot Racing Cat	1.00
How to Build a Flattie or Sharpie	1.25
How to Build an Ice-Yacht—with Building Plans of a Scooter	.75
How to Build a Knockabout	.75
How to Build a Model Yacht	1.25
How to Build a Motor Launch	.50
How to Build a Racer for $50..........paper 75c; Cloth	1.00
How to Build a Rowboat	1.25
How to Build a Skipjack	.75
How to Build a Small Cruising Power Boat	.25
How to Build a Speed Launch	1.00
How to Build a 32-Foot Cruising Launch. By H. L. Skene	1.00
How to Build V-Bottom Boats	1.25
How to Build a Viper	.25
How to Design and Construct a Power Boat	2.00
How to Design a Yacht. By C. G. Davis	2.00
How to Run a Boat Shop. By Desmond	1.25
How to Run and Install a Gasolene Engine. By C. Von Culin	.25
How Sails Are Made and Handled. By C. G. Davis	2.00
Boatbuilders' Estimating Pads	1.25
Boat Building and Boating. By Beard	1.35
Boating Book for Boys	1.50
Motor Boats, Construction and Operation	1.50
Steel Shipbuilders' Handbook. An Encyclopedia. By C. W. Cook	1.50

GAS ENGINES

Diesel Engines, Marine and Stationary. By A. H. Goldingham	3.00
Elements of Gas Engine Design	.75
Gas Engine Handbook. By Roberts. 7th Edition	2.00
Gas Engines. By Lieckfeldt	.25
Gas, Gasolene and Oil Engines. By Gardner D. Hiscox	3.00
How to Run and Install a Gasolene Engine. By Von Culin	.25
Marine Gas Engines. By Clark	2.00
Motor Boats, Construction and Operation	1.25
Oil Engines. By A. H. Goldingham	2.50
Questions and Answers from the Gas Engine	1.50
Resistance of Ships and Screw Propulsion	2.25
Valves and Valve Gears for Gasolene, Gas and Oil Engines: Part I, $2.50; Part II,	2.00

DESIGNS

RUDDER WHAT TO BUILD SERIES—

Cabin Plan Book	$1.00	Racer Book	$1.00
Cat Book...........paper	.50	Schooner Book	1.25
Power Cruiser Book	1.00	Yawl Book...........paper	.75

ICE-BOATS

How to Build an Ice-Yacht—with Building Plans of a Scooter	.75

YACHT AND NAVAL ARCHITECTURE

Naval Architecture Simplified. By Chas. Desmond	5.00
A Text Book of Laying Off. By Atwood and Cooper	2.25
Elements of Yacht Design. By N. L. Skene	2.00
Handbook of Ship Calculations, Construction and Operation	5.25
Laying Down and Taking Off. By Desmond	2.00
Machinery's Handbook	6.00
Manual of Yacht and Boat Sailing and Yacht Architecture. Kemp	15.00
Naval Architects' Pocket Book. By MacKrow	6.00
Naval Architecture. A Manual of Laying-Off. By Watson	12.00
Naval Architecture. By Peabody	7.50
Naval Constructor. By Simpson	5.00
Practical Shipbuilding. By A. C. Holms. 3d Edition	20.00
Practical Shipfitting. By Shi-Dk	2.00
Practical Ship Production. By Carmichael	3.00
Speed and Power of Ships. 2 Vols. By Taylor	7.50
Tables for Constructing Ships' Lines. By Hogg	1.00
The Power Boat, Its Construction and Design. By Schock	2.00
Theoretical Naval Architecture. By Atwood	3.50
Wooden Shipbuilding. By Desmond	10.00

ELECTRICAL

Dry Batteries. By a Dry Battery Expert	.35
Electrical Circuits and Diagrams. By N. H. Schneider	.35
Electric Wiring, Diagrams and Switchboards. By Newton Harrison	1.50
Electric Bells and Alarms	.35
Induction Coils. By P. Marshall	.35
Modern Primary Batteries	.35
Practical Electrics	.35
Small Accumulators. By Marshall	.35
Study of Electricity. By Schneider	.35

MODEL YACHTS

How to Build a Model Yacht	1.25
Building Model Boats. By P. N. Hasluck	.75
Machinery for Model Steamers	.35
Model Engines and Small Boats. By Hopkins	1.25
Model Sailing Yachts. By Marshall	.75

MARINE ENGINEERING

Calculus for Engineers. By Larkman	2.00
Elements of Mechanism. By Schwamb	2.50
New Marine Engineers' Guide	3.00
Marine Propellers. By Barnaby	5.00
Marine Steam Turbine. By J. W. Sothern. 3d Edition	15.00
Manual of Marine Engineering. By Seaton	10.00
Mechanics' and Engineers' Pocketbook. By Charles H. Haswell	5.00
Practical Marine Engineering. By Capt. C. W. Dyson, U. S. N.	6.00

NAVIGATION

Navigation Simplified. By McArthur	1.25
American Practical Navigator. Bowditch........$2.25; by mail	2.50
American Nautical Almanac	.30
Navigation—A Short Course. By Hasting	.75
Navigation. By G. L. Hosmer	1.25
Modern Navigation. By Hastings	.75
Self Instructor in Navigation	3.00
Simple Rules and Problems in Navigation	4.00
Elements of Navigation. By Henderson	1.25
Epitome of Navigation. By Norie..............2 Vols.	15.00
Navigation. By Jacoby	2.25
Navigators' Pocket Book. By Capt. Howard Patterson	2.00
Practical Aid to the Navigator. By Sturdy	2.00
Wrinkles in Practical Navigation. By Lecky	5.00
Book of Sights Taken in Actual Practice at Sea	1.00
Brown's Star Atlas	2.00
Deviation and Deviascope	2.00
Manual on Rules of the Road at Sea	3.25
Pocket Course Book Chesapeake Bay	.25
Pocket Course Book Long Island Sound	.25
Pocket Course Book New England Waters	.25
Pocket Course Book Portland to Halifax	.25
Pocket Course Book Race Rock to Boston Light	.25

PUGSLEY'S—

Dead Reckoning	2.25
Latitude by Meridian Altitude	2.25
Learners' Compass Card	.85
Guide to the Local Inspectors' Examination—Ocean Going Steam and Sail	2.25
New York Pilot and Guide to the Local Inspectors' Examination	2.25
Log Book	2.25
Multiplication Table	1.15
Seaman's Receipt Book	.35
Tides	2.25
Handy Jack Book of Navigation Tables..............paper	.75
Ex-Meridian, Altitude, Azimuth and Star Finding Tables	3.15
Tables for Correcting the Observed Altitude, etc. By S. Anfindsen	1.00

THE RUDDER

Single Copies, 25c; Monthly, a Year	2.00
Bound Volumes: 1910, 1911, 1916, 1917, 1918	4.00
Covers for Binding	1.25

Prices Subject to Change.

ABOVE PRICES INCLUDE DELIVERY ONLY WITHIN THE UNITED STATES. PURCHASERS IN FOREIGN COUNTRIES MUST ADD 25 PER CENT TO AMOUNT OF ORDER TO COVER DELIVERY.

The Rudder Publishing Company, 9 Murray St., New York, N. Y.

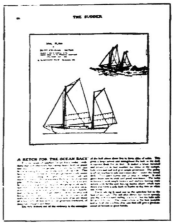